Ways of Old

Growing Up in the Needmore/Hightower Community - Bryson City, NC

By

Bonnie Lou Cochran

Bonnie Lou Cochran,
May God Bless you!
5-23-06

authorHOUSE™

1663 LIBERTY DRIVE, SUITE 200
BLOOMINGTON, INDIANA 47403
(800) 839-8640
WWW.AUTHORHOUSE.COM

First published by AuthorHouse 01/04/06

ISBN: 1-4208-8843-9 (sc)

Library of Congress Control Number: 2005908680

Printed in the United States of America
Bloomington, Indiana

This book is printed on acid-free paper.

DEDICATION:

I would like to dedicate this book to my family. First to my husband, Raymond for being so patient with me during the time I have spent at the computer writing the stories, and for being my best friend.

To my wonderful children; Kevin, and wife Mary and Granddaughter Mayson, Chris and wife Angela, Grandson David and Granddaughter Mellanie. I want you guys to keep yesteryear alive and pass on the "Ways of Old" to future generations.

To my Mom (The Walking and Talking Farmers Almanac), Pauline Dehart Sutton. Thank you Mom for teaching me to have faith in God, and for being my Almanac all these years. To my Brothers and Sisters also Emma and Kim.

In loving memory of my Dad, Luther Martin Sutton, My Grandma Pearl Ann Potts Wikle Dehart, Uncle Lloyd Sutton and Aunt Ollie Parton Bailey.

My Mentors, Aunt Edna Sutton, Harrie and Dessie Parton and Faye Cochran Along with my parents and Grandma who have taught me to live by the Ways of Old.

Most of all I want to thank God for bringing to my remembrance the events of the stories. With out Him I am nothing. One of my favorite verses is "I am thy God: I will strengthen thee: Yea, I will help thee"...... Isaiah 41-10

The people who encouraged me the most to write this book were my two Brothers; Marvin and Charles Sutton, wife Jennifer, and Emma Waldroup. Thank you all for your support.

TABLE OF CONTENTS

SECTION ONE:
COMMUNITY AND FAMILY

MY BABY BROTHER

This story is a tribute to my baby brother, Charles Jesse Sutton. Charles arrived on a hot July day back in 1950. This day is my earliest childhood memory. I had turned two years old the last day of February being a little over four months before my Brother was born.

My Daddy was out in the wood shed moaning and groaning, repeatedly vomiting. The Doctor was "sent for". He arrived not to see my Daddy but to help with the delivery of my Brother. My Aunt Edna was at the house too. (Both my parents have said that my Daddy had the labor pains when Charles was born).

My older Brother, Marvin who was nearly two years older than me, My Uncle Lloyd, his daughter Emma who was a month younger than Marvin and I went on an adventure walk. This was planned to keep us kids away from the house for a while. We walked through the pasture where the cows were grazing, hunting for treasures. After what seemed a long time, clad with our many different rock finds, our hands stained from picking and eating blackberries found along the way, we arrived back at the house. My Daddy seemed just fine. The Doctor was still at the house waiting for my Grandma to fix the evening meal.

In the bed with my Mama was a new baby boy. Charles was late in arriving (post dates of over two weeks). The Baby was all arms and legs, skinny legs and a big head. I wanted to know where he came from? His name was Charles Jesse Sutton. The Charles part was after my Mama's father being Charlie Dehart. The Jesse part was after my Daddy's father being Jess Sutton.

My Grandma Pearl was in the kitchen preparing the meal. She needed another pot, which was stored under a small table in the kitchen. Grandma asked me to get the pot for her; I reached into the storage space and retrieved the pot. I felt something bite my finger. I brought the pot and my hand out. On my finger was a spider. I was screaming, jumping up and down making a big fuss. The Doctor came into the kitchen to see what in the world was taking place. He removed the spider from my finger, washed the finger with alcohol and applied some iodine. He assured all of us that the spider was not a poisonous one; He said I would be all right. I was. I have always been a little scared of spiders.

The scrawny baby took my bed. I had been sleeping with Mama and now the "new baby" was in my bed. I was not happy at all and had to sleep with my Grandma. I did not like that one bit. As a matter of fact I didn't like that scrawny baby at all. After awhile I got used to sleeping with Grandma. I kinda got used to the baby. He would smile at me and make funny noises. I started liking him.

By the time my first sister was born, three years later, Charles and I were big buddies. I was glad he had to give up the bed to another "new baby", served him right. As we grew up Charles was a real quite child. He was small for his age, which may be why the other boys always picked on him. He was so good natured. He never got upset or showed any anger. I would really get on to him to take up for himself. He would say, "Sis don't get so upset, it will be OK". We moved from below the Hightower Church to Wiggins Creek which is still in the Needmore Community before Charles turned four.

Our neighbors the Fred Ammons family lived up the road and the Wayne Ammons family lived down the road. Fred had three boys and three girls. Wayne had four boys and one girl. My two brothers and all the other boys made a total of nine boys within three tents of a mile. Harold was a little younger than me and Edwin was close to Charles's age. Steven was younger. Rhoda was younger, she was closer to my sister's age. There was Francis who was older than Marvin. J.T. was close to Marvin's age. Joe was close to my age. Billy and Neil were younger Wayne and Fred were brothers, making all the Ammons kids first cousins. Merrill Ammons was my Daddy's sister; she married Wayne. We were first cousins to their kids, but no relation to Fred's family.

Time passed swiftly, all the kids were growing. In the summers the kids mingled between the houses to play.

The boys would all get together and play softball in the pasture. Another thing they liked to play was on the red clay bank across the road from our house. They build little roads all along the bank. The dozer was a sharp rock scooted through the dirt to move the dirt for their roads. Most of the cars used were homemade make do's. If any one had a store bought car; it was considered a treasure and closely guarded. The boys did not allow me to play with the cars and roads, unless of course there were no neighbor kids around, and then Charles wanted me to play cars with him. My Mama was sick with a heart condition when we were growing up. She could look out the window or door and see the kids playing on the road bank and did not have to holler to know where they were playing.

The other game, which was a "boys only" game, was shooting marbles. I was not allowed to touch their marbles. I would go by the area where they were playing and occasionally collect a stray marble. I never understood that game. I still do not know the game. A big circle was drawn in the sand (our drive way was the place of choice. The likelihood of a car coming onto our driveway was scarce to none.

The Wayne Ammons family soon moved to Conleys Creek at Whittier, which was about twenty five miles away. Back then it seemed a world away to us kids. We missed them so much. We only saw them at church on Sunday and very rare occasions otherwise.

The new neighbors who moved into the house where Wayne's family moved from, was Violet and Vance Winchester. They had three girls, younger than me, but we became fast friends. It kinda evened out the female population in the community. Their names were Cathy, Sandy and Arlene. Later Ervin and Mike came along. They lived in the community for several years. We spent many hours together. Violet and Vance were no relation to us, but treated us like family. I still cherish both of them today.

Charles acquired a nickname as a small boy. Our family consumed a large amount of pinto beans in the winter time. Charles loved to eat those beans. Charles was prone to having a flatulent stomach at any given time. This was an inherited trait and was a prized possession to a young mountain boy. Pinto beans and sweet potatoes were the finest of fuel for activation. Riding the school bus on the following morning after the consumption of one of the previous mentioned foods could become quiet interesting or disgusting. Clyde Breedlove (Cora's Clyde) had taken on the roll of mentor and correctional officer for Charles. Clyde started calling him "Beanie" in relation to the distinctive odor following Charles. The name stuck. Some of the family still call Charles "Beanie" to this day.

My brother remained calm and easy going all through the years. We shared some really great times together. As I got older, he was my chaperone. Charles loved to skate. There was a local skating rink just opened in the area. I had my driver's license, if I went any where in the car Charles had to go. I would pay his way to skate for a few hours and I either skated or road around in the car. He was so easy to talk into doing what I wanted.

Charles is still that same easygoing fellow of long ago. He still has the patience of Job. I learned to love him soon after he was born and that hasn't changed. I love you Charles.

Some of the information in this story will be repeated in other stories.

THE HIGHTOWER / NEEDMORE COMMUNITY

The Needmore Community got its name not after a persons name but because of a saying. Mrs. Ester Dehart Burnette (Lawter's) father Andrew Jackson Dehart and a bunch of men were working across the Little Tennessee River. This was a very long time ago; the people of the community had been trying to think up a name for the community. While the men were working across the river, they kept running out of supplies to build with and feed for the animals. The men would holler across the river for some other men to bring the supplies over from the store. "We need more" Every day they would holler "We need more". The men decided that would be a good name for the community. It was submitted to the county officials and was awarded the Needmore Community. (This was told to me by Mrs. Ester Lawter who is now one hundred and one years old being the oldest living member of the community today, as I am writing this story.) One other story was rumored that the need in the community was always so great that they always did need more of everything.

We were living down by the Little Tennessee River in the old Pearson Dehart house that sat right above the state road. The Needmore Swinging Bridge was located just below our house on the left. There was a rock quarry on the right side of the road at the bridge. Across the bridge and to the left a little ways lived U.Z. and Dorothy (Dot) Burnette with their family. Pat, Bill, Judy and Becky. U.Z.'s mother, Ester lived there also and managed the U.S. Post Office. That is where we got our mail along with every one else. No mail carrier at that time. There were rumors of a rural route being started for the Needmore area and doing away with the Post Office. Mrs. Ester Burnette gave the position over to Dot and moved to Winston Salem to look for work. The Brush Creek Baptist Church was on down the road. That is as far as we went in that direction.

Up the road to the right of the bridge on the same side of the river was the Doyle and Mellie Hampton place. Their children were Georgia Lee and Paul, and maybe others . Back across the bridge on the edge of the river was the old Grist Mill. That is where everyone went to have his or her corn ground. On down the road on the left hand side was where Uncle Harvey and Aunt Laura Simmonds lived. (They were not really our aunt and uncle, that's what all elderly people were called back then). The Simmonds children were Earnest who owned a little Country Store just below their house, Hoyt, Joyce, and Irene that I remember. There may have been others. Aunt Laura Simmonds was a delightful plump little lady. They moved from the community when I was about eight or nine years old. I remember that my Daddy bought the only doll I ever owned at Earn's store. A variety of things could be bought at the store. Just around the curve was a little house where my brother Charles was born, we did not live there long. We then moved into the house described above. No other houses were below until you passed the Wiggins Creek Road and Luther and Florence Phillips lived off to the left up a dirt road a little ways. After The Simmonds family moved away Lon Dehart, his wife Stella and children, Helen, Clifford, Clayton and Ferman moved into the same house. The store was torn down.

Up the road from our house the first driveway to the left and a ways off the main road lived Aunt Lisa Simmonds, her daughter Aunt Mary Dehart. Aunt Mary's daughter Olive Franks lived just below them. Olive's children's names are Bill, Jean, Brenda and Buddy. Aunt Lisa was a devout Christian woman. She believed that God would drop her a piece of corn bread from heaven before He would allow her to starve. We called her Aunt Leasy. Her daughter, Aunt Mary was equally sweet and wonderful.

Next and very soon on the left was where Henry and Alice Posey lived. Their children were Joyce, Etta Mae, Geraldine, Douglas, Alfred (Cotton), and Barbara. Barbara was the same age as my brother Marvin. My real Uncle Everett Wikle lived directly above the Hightower Baptist Church. The church was in the same building as the Hightower School had been. The Wikle children were Joyce, Calvin, Iris and Charles. My Uncle was raising his children alone.

There were no Hightowers living in the area. The Hightower School (as rumor went) was named after the first teacher who started teaching school in the one room old school which originated on the old Wikle place. At the Register of Deeds in Bryson City there is no record of any Hightower owning land in the Needmore Community. Mrs Ester Dehart Burnette Lawter does not remember hearing the teachers name or how the school got started. The original one room school was located on the Wikle old home place below where my Mama was raised. Mrs. Lawter attended school at the old school before it "burned to the ground". After the school burned the new school was built on Bob Breedloves property. The new Hightower School held classes from first through the fifth grade. The other kids were transported to the old Almond School. The Hightower School resolved in 1938 or 1939. The old Almond School was located where the Almond Boat Dock is now. When the Fontana Dam was built The Almond School was torn down and some of the materials were used in the building of the new Almond School located at Lauada. The new school opened in 1945 with grades 1 through 8. The new Almond School accommodated kids from several neighborhood schools. The kids in grades 9 through 12 attended the Swain County High School. The last graduating class at the old Almond School was 1944, the year my Mama and Aunt Edna graduated from the

11th grade. There was no graduating class of 1945 because the 12th grade was added. A lot of change took place in the schools of Swain County that year.

Church was held in the school on Sunday mornings and continued after the school closed. Bob Breedlove sold the property to Ray Dehart. Ray Dehart later sold the property to the community. In 1958 the property was ordained as Hightower Baptism Church.

On up the road past Lick Log Creek Road, I will go there in a bit; the first drive to the right and a ways back was where Clyde and Flossie Breedlove lived. They were delightful people, who owned a chicken farm. Aunt Flossie gave me a pet chicken. I feed the chicken and took good care of her. The Breedlove's had no children.

Back out to the road and immediately to the left and a good ways from the road lived Author and Sarah Breedlove. Mr. Author gave me a silver dollar the day I was born, I still have it. Their children were Dorothy (Dot Brunette, married to U.Z.) Don, Odell, Wanda, Dean and Billy. There may have been others. My Mama went to school with Dorothy.

On down the road and just below the Windy Gap Cemetery lived Hance and Selma Ammons. Their daughter Jean was my brother Marvin's age. They also had a son named Odell, one named Don and two other girls, Alene and Berda. Hance built a new house up in the hollow and to the right of where he lived. After a few years Hance sold to Cecil and Francis Dorsey with daughters Vickie and Donna. Across the road from the cemetery and to the right was Long Branch road. My real Uncle Adam and Aunt Elvira,(we called her Aunt Vary and still do,) lived in a big long house with a wrap-around porch. Their children's names are Loutena, Arnold, Mildred, May Lee, Maxine, Arley (R. L.), Barbara, Marie and Shirley. Later Robert (Bobby) and Becky were added to the family. I loved spending the night at their home, there was so much excitement, and all the bigger kids petted the smaller ones. I was close to Marie's age.

On down the road where the road meets the river, there was a driveway that went to the right, called Rattle Snake Creek Road, (named for a reason I am sure.) A good long ways up the road lived my real Aunt Rosie Dyer and husband Uncle Will. They are mentioned in another story. Their children were all grown. A son named Wayne, and two daughters. Jessie who had a daughter named Carolyn, and Lucille whose children were Imogene, Reba, Glenda, and later boys named, John and Mike. Geraldine whose children were Linton, Clinton, and Linda Brooks. I loved my Aunt Rosie so very much. She was a beautiful woman and so sweet. When you received a hug from aunt Rosie you were hugged all over. Just above their house was my Grandpa Jess and Granny Mary Loucinda Ball Sutton. I inherited the Lou from her name. Their place was a beautiful place. The only bad part was the creek crossed the road sixteen times between the main road and their house. There was always a big bunch of people at their house. My Uncle Claude and Uncle Odell were the only ones still at home unmarried. My Grandpa was always wearing bib overalls. My Granny was a very little woman with black hair pulled back and fastened at the back of her head. As Grandpa's health became worse they sold and moved closer into town. My Grandparents both died the same year. I was 10 years old. Such a tragedy. My Granny fell in the floor and hit her head. She died from the fall. My grandpa had died a few months before from deteriorating health. My Daddy's family was devastated.

Back down the road toward the Hightower Church to the left was Lick Log Creek. There was an old house at the beginning of the road. On up the road to the left and up on a hill lived the Golden's. Their niece was Rebecca Waldroup. They didn't live there long. On up the road was a big beautiful white house owned by Uncle Bob Breedlove, a widower. The same Bob Breedlove who allowed the school to be built on his property. His children were all grown. One daughter, Chloe and husband Tob and son Bobby lived just above Uncle Bob. Uncle Bob loved gospel music better than any thing. After he got home bound different people went to sing for him. Away from the road and above him another son lived, Thad and wife Evaneil and daughter Donna. Other children were Max, Gilmer and another daughter.

Farther up the road was the Posey place. Mr. And Mrs. Andy Posey and their son Lee and wife Patty and four daughters. The Posey's had to relocate from the Bushnell area with my Daddy's Family.

The daughters were Donna, Florence, Dorothy who was my age and in my class at school, my friend, and Reona a year younger. Later two name carriers were added. Nathan and Jackson. Burlin Posey, brother to Lee had a place across the field.

At the end of the state maintained road lived Uncle John and Aunt Ella (Eller) Breedlove. This couple loved for kids to visit them. They had no children of their own but did have nieces and nephews. Up the dirt road a ways lived a widow with her children. Florence Breedlove had Curtice, twins Jay Hill and Faye Hilda (I may have the names reversed), Nevil who was my age and in my grade at school. Most people called him Breedlove. Then there was Ann and Kathy. If ever a place should have a name earned that place would have been Copperhead Hollow. I was scared to death to walk up their road. Florence found a copperhead in her kitchen one time I was there. Florence was a petite plump lady with a big hearty laugh. She just got rid of the snake and didn't make much of a fuss. I loved to hear her laugh.

Now back to the Hightower Church and to the direct left onto Hightower Road and down that road a ways when starting up the hill on the right was my birthplace. Directly below and on below the road was where my parents were building a new house. The same place as the Old Hightower School before the school burned. The creek was close by and the spring a little farther away. A short distance up the road was where my real Uncle Lloyd and Aunt Edna lived with their daughter Emma. Later in life another daughter was born to them named Kimberly Dawn. The next house up the road was where Mrs. Cora Breedlove lived with her son Clyde and daughter Betty. Other children's names were Lee, Frank, Grace (who was married to Jessie Davis and lived up above Cora with children Gary and Marie. Later Cindy came along.) Bethel and Gladys who had moved from here. Thelma who was married to Fred Ammons and lived on over on Wiggins Creek.

There is a long steep drive down hill past Jessie's that connected to Wiggins Creek Road. A little ways beyond was the old Jeff Wikle place. The old two-story farmhouse sat empty at the time. The road forked. To the right and up the road lived a widower named Mose Wikle. A small framed man who was so wonderful with us kids. His children were married and gone from home. One daughter was Maude Burgan and husband Wayne with children Carolyn and Bud. The other one was Neil Hayes. Mr. Wikle was a devout Christian man who walked to the Maple Springs Baptist Church every Sunday morning and was cherished by all who knew him. We kids loved this little man. Mr. Wikle will be mentioned again in another story.

Back up the left side of the road a little ways was where my real Aunt Merrill and Uncle Wayne Ammons lived. We bought their place in a few years. Their children were Francis, J.T., Joe who was close to my age; Billy Wayne and Neil were younger. Above them lived Uncle Wayne's brother Fred and Thelma Ammons, mentioned before, as Thelma was Cora Breedlove's daughter. Their children were Harold who was one year younger than me, Edwin who was my brother Charles's age, Rhoda, Freda, and later Stephen and Deloris. Back down the road to the forks of the road where Hightower Road met Wiggins Creek Road and around a couple of curves was a little house on the left where Frank and Ann (her real name was Arvella) Breedlove lived. They later built a house above ours and below Fred's. The children were Deloris and Dianne and later four more children. On below them and up a steep road to the left was where Glen and Mae Breedlove lived. Their youngest child was Jean, my brother Marvin's age. There was Alvin and wife Maude who built a house above Glen and a few years later had two daughters Carol Lynn and Karen. Glen's other daughters were Violent, Bobby and Tina. There will be more about Violent later. Down the main road a good long ways was where Carl and Nan Jones lived with their family. Opal was probably gone from home by now. There were Betty Jean (her son James), Kenneth, Ray, Rachel who was closer to my age, Melvin (who much later became my brother-in-law, married my sister Dianne). The younger ones were Ruth and Ann.

That was the end of Wiggins Creek Road. I am now back to the river and where Luther Phillips lived. On down the road by the river, in a big two story farm house lived Preacher John Freeman and family. Ann and Roger were still at home. Spurgeon and Bill were gone from home. Bill (her real name is Delma) was married to Wifford Johnson who lived on up the road above Ralph Breedlove's store.

There may have been other Freeman kids. Between the Freeman's and the store was a couple named Oscar and Lula Sanders who had no children. Now we are to Ralph and Dess Breedlove (who owned the little country store, which was appreciated by all), and children Paul and Arnold who were gone from home. Margaret was married to Stanley Bailey and lived up on Panther (Painter) Branch who later had Dawn and Terry Bailey. Ralph and Dess's other children were Dean and David. We are back to Wiff and Bill Johnson's place. They had a daughter a few years later. You have never seen prouder parents. They named their little girl Sherry. We kids pestered Bill to death to get to hold Sherry.

On up the road in a big white frame house lived Troy and Maude Allen. They had grown children. One son who was named Clyde. Dessie who was married to Harrie Parton (these people became my in-laws much later). There were Gertrude, Helen and Mary Ellen. Above their house was the Maple Springs Church. That was as far as we were allowed to walk.

Back down the road just past Ralph's Store and to the right was Panther Branch Road. The first house on that road was home to Obie and Grace McCall. They had six boys. Dewey, my age Emmett, Danny, Bruce, Obie Lee, and Johnny. On up the road a little ways was where Stanley and Margaret Bailey lived, mentioned before.(Margaret was Ralph and Dess Breedlove's daughter). A drive directly across from Stanley's was where Norman and Ethel Simonds Breedlove lived.

Their children were Janice, Patty and Carolyn. Jerry came later. Just above Stanley's was where his grandparents lived Mr. and Mrs Bailey. Stanley was their "boy". Above their house a road went to the right. Harrie Parton owned some land and at the end of the road was the Sitton Place. Mrs. Sitton (a widow) was away up in years as were the Bailey's just mentioned. Mrs. Sitton lived alone on the big beautiful farm. Her children were married and gone from home.

Back on the main road to the left, up the road a little ways was a drive off to the left. Up on the hill Bill and Lilly Bailey lived with children Dorothy, Jack, and Charles. Bill was Stanley's dad. Mr. And Mrs. Bailey mentioned before were Bill's parents. The next house up the main road was home to Preacher Jim Simonds, wife and family. Mrs. Simonds had suffered and survived from a serious stroke. She was in a wheel chair. Their children were Ethel Breedlove, married to Norman, living down the road. Ray, Sue, J. C. and Don. Don was my brother Marvin's friend. There may have been more children. Don was just a small kid when his mother had the stroke. Most stroke victims did not live back then. Mr. And Mrs. Simonds were the kindest of people. Mr. Simonds looked after his wife and farmed tobacco. The children helped care for their mother while Mr. Simonds worked in the tobacco field and did odd jobs for other farmers. Mrs. Simonds was so fragile looking. It broke my heart to see her in the wheel chair. A sweeter woman was never to be found. We kids liked to push her wheel chair in and out of the church when we attended Maple Springs Baptist.

Up the road a little ways from the Simonds' place was the old Breedlove place. Ralph, Glen and Norman's Daddy lived there He was well up in years also. Just above his house the school bus turned around. On past the "the turn-around" a little ways was where Lessie Cunningham lived with daughters Mary John and Faye. Faye was Marvin's age. Her other daughters Bernice and Claudell were married. Claudell and husband Dan Wike lived on up the road. Ralph Breedlove owned a house above Claudell. Ken Mar Estate was on top of the mountain (which might still have belonged to Ralph Breedlove at that time.)

I have mentioned the entire Needmore Community with part of the Maple Springs Community and Panther (Painter) Branch. The Needmore road meets the main highway U.S. 19.

My family moved onto the Hightower Road (which did not have a name back then) in the new house and lived there about three years, The TVA was planning to build a dam on the Little Tennessee River. My Daddy's family had been removed from their property down at Eagle Bluff when the Fontana Dam was being built. My parents decided to sell their place. They bought the place where My Uncle Wayne and Aunt Merrill Ammons lived. My Aunt and Uncle moved into the Jeff Wikle place and lived there a short time. They then moved to Conley's Creek, at Whittier, N. C. a whole world away from Needmore, or so it seemed to us kids. Vance and Violet

Winchester (she was a daughter of Glen and Mae Breedlove) moved into the Jeff Wikle place after the Ammon's family moved away.

My uncle Adam Sutton and family moved into the Freeman place down on the river after a few years. These were the people I was acquainted with while growing up in the Hightower Needmore Community. We knew we had relatives living in other parts of the country due to the "move" making room for the Fontana Lake. Some we saw occasionally, others we never knew what happened to them.

GOING TO GRANDPA AND GRANNY SUTTON'S

My Grandparents had been forced to leave their home at Eagle Bluff, Bushnell N.C. in 1944 so as to make room for the Fontana Lake. Of course this was before I was born. Actually it was before my parents met. The new Jess Sutton home was in the Needmore Community, about a mile or so up a dirt road that crossed the Rattle Snake Creek sixteen times before reaching to their house. I'm told the Creek was named a long time before, true to its naming because of the abundance of Rattle Snakes. This was mentioned in the previous story. Please excuse the repetitions, as some of the stories were written as just a story and later became part of this book.

My parents met shortly after the move. My Mother was born and raised in the Needmore Community, not far from the Hightower Church, which was not a church but a school during that time. My mother attended school there while growing up. Her parents were

Pearl Ann Potts Wikle Dehart A second marriage for her and a third marriage for my Grandpa Charlie Samuel Dehart. My Grandma Pearl Potts was from Macon County and married Bill Wikle the first time and they had five children, Nancy, Everett, Mae, Maude and Earl. (Earl was killed at age 19.) My Grandma was a widow when she met Charlie Dehart. The Deharts lived-in the Needmore Community with relatives in surrounding Communities and also had relatives in Graham County. There were several off springs from his two previous marriages.

My Granny Sutton (Mary Loucinda Ball) was from Bryson City, formerly known as Charleston. The Suttons were from Bushnell and surrounding areas. They had produced a very large family. My Daddy had eight brothers and five sisters; He was fifth from the youngest.

On August 12 th, 1945 My Mother Pauline Dehart and my Daddy Luther Martin Sutton were joined in marriage in Georgia. An all day trip there and back. My brother Marvin Lee Sutton was born in May 1946. February 1948 I Bonnie Lou made my first appearance into this world. July 1950 my brother Charles Jesse Sutton was born. Linda Faye was born September 1953. And Dianne was born in August 1955. My maternal Grandfather died before my parents were married. My Grandma Pearl lived with us. I guess I should say we lived with her. When Mama and Daddy got married, Daddy moved in with Mama and Grandma. When my parents moved Grandma moved with them.

It was like having two Mamas.

When we were small we lived a ways below the Hightower Church. The only way to visit my Grandparents was to walk. We did just that occasionally. The long walk to the Jess Sutton home took some time. We would usually go on a Saturday or Sunday evening. There were only three of us kids at this time. Foot Logs were used for crossing the creek on foot (a big log was placed across the creek for a walk way) We kids didn't mind getting our feet wet in the summer, we enjoyed wading the creek. Any cars or trucks traveling the road had to ford the creek, meaning there was no bridge. There was a beautiful set of falls at the top of the hill, cascading water 35 or 40 feet over a giant rock cliff. The large creek held Native Trout and several kinds of Minnows. Occasionally we would get a glimpse of the trout if the water was clear and we were very quiet.

The hill by the falls was very hard to climb. We kids got tired walking so far. My Daddy would get a kid under each arm and carry us up the hill. My Mother would carry Charles, the baby at that time. I thought my Daddy was the strongest man in the world. It sure felt good to be carried. Sometimes Mama and Charles stayed at home. Other times He would stay with my Grandma.

After more walking and crossing the creek we finally came to my Aunt Rosie Dyers house. Aunt Rosie was married to Will Dyer. They had three older children. The next house was Grandpas. There was a log bridge, (not a foot log) across the creek. The bridge was several logs connected together making a wide bridge. The barn sat on the side of the creek next to the road. The house was across the creek away from the road. To the left after crossing the creek was a very large Hemlock tree. Underneath the tree was a spring house. The spring over flow water ran through the spring house. There was a spring box, long and narrow made from wood, which held glass jars of sweet milk, buttermilk, cream, butter and apple cider. The cold spring water filled the box, keeping the items listed cool. There was another bigger box filled with the water flowing from the spring box, which could cool a watermelon just perfect. A few wooden chairs took up residence there as well as a few blocks of wood used to sit up on. On very hot days this was a refuge from the heat, the building was made of wooden slats about 2 inches apart, thus allowing for air circulation. The cool creek near by and the spring water added to the coolness of the area. Occasionally the men could be found here, sipping homemade whisky. The family tradition of the times. A tin roof overhead, and a door to keep animals out completed the spring house.

The log house had a porch the entire length of the front of the house. Rock steps underneath a canopy of Hemlock Trees led up to the porch. The door was about one third way down the porch that led into the Front Room (now called the living room). On the right was a set of steps leading to the upstairs bedrooms. To the left of the door was a sofa. Farther down the room was a full size bed and directly across the room was another bed. A couple of chairs, a dresser and a smaller table completed the room, except for the fireplace, which was in the wall next to the stairs. In cool weather a fire was always aglow. A big cast iron pot of pinto beans were cooking in the fireplace. The house had a side room, back room and kitchen with a dining room besides the living room. In the kitchen were a wood burning cook stove, a small table, wood box, and a cupboard. If there were not beans cooking in the fireplace there were beans cooking on the back of the wood cook stove. This stove helped to heat the house during cold weather along with the open fireplace. There was a warmer shelf above the cook stove where left over food was stored and kept warm for hours. The water supply was a ten-quart bucket with a dipper used by every one to drink water. The water was carried from the spring. Just outside the kitchen was a small porch with a wash pan, soap, and water sitting on the plank anchored onto the wall and again to the post beside the step. A towel was hanging on a nail. This was where washing of the hands took place before the meals. Also shaving was done here. A small mirror was tacked to the wall. No bathroom. An out side toilet sat a little ways from the house. The plank holding the wash pan was also where Granny cooled her pies and cakes.

Various shrubs were growing around the house and lots of pink roses. The garden was above the house. Free-range chickens were scratching in the yard. A dog lay lazily on the front porch. A pigpen held a fattening hog. A cow grazed on the hill along side a horse. The barn was filled with hay. A corncrib held corn for the farm animals and also for the family's corn bread and hominy. A sack of corn was taken to the mill, which was located right below our house. The corn was ground into meal, the person grinding the corn kept some out for himself as pay for grinding. Corn meal mush was also made from the ground corn as well as meal used for frying fish and other foods. To make mush a pot of water with a little salt was boiled on the stove. A cup or so of meal was stirred into the boiling water and continued to cook until smooth. This was served in a bowl with milk poured over the mush, or honey poured on top (with out the milk) with a big glob of butter. This was sometimes the evening meal. A big lunch was served at noon (called dinner, the evening meal was called supper.)

There were two uncles not married still living at home, along with several relatives living close by, so usually a crowd of people were at Granny's house. My Granny was a very small woman, under five feet and not weighing a hundred pounds with her hair pulled back and fastened to her head. We usually ate something before we left. Grandpa was not a real large man but much larger than Granny. He always wore bib overhauls. They would wave to us as we started on our journey back home. Some how the distance seemed shorter on the return route, especially since most of the way was down hill.

My Grand Parents sold their place and moved closer in toward town due to declining health. They both died the same year, just a few months apart. The old home place has changed dramatically since then. Memories of my childhood often take me back to the beautiful creek and the cool spring box. These memories will always be alive in my heart.

THE NEEDMORE SWINGING BRIDGE

While living near the Little Tennessee River in the Needmore Community we got our mail at the Post Office across the river. We walked across the swinging bridge to get there and back. Mrs. Ester Burnett was the Post Master.

A swinging bridge (Webster Dictionary) a bridge that swings freely from or on a support. As you walked on the bridge it would sway and bobble, this can be quiet scary to people who aren't familiar with crossing such a bridge. It took a long time for me to get comfortable walking the bridge.

The bridge was made with two large steel posts in the ground at three different places. At the beginning, in the middle (at the Island), and at the other side making six of the very tall steel posts. Big steel cables were connected to the steel posts. The bridge was constructed of long boards (called planks back then.) The bridge was about three feet wide; so several rows of the long boards were used. Smaller cables were connected to the wooden part of the bridge and connected to the top bigger cables that reached from steel post to steel post. The cables were high on the ends and lower in the middle, thus creating an arch. A continuous row of four feet high garden wire was connected on both sides of the bridge in order to prevent people from falling or jumping into the river.

The bottom of an Island ended just under the bridge, dividing the river with more river toward the road. Like 2/5 and 3/5. There were steps from the bridge to the Island but you had to climb over the garden wire. The Island was a good place to play ball. There was a lot of sand and not much vegetation. An occasional soft ball was lost to the river and carried away by the current before it could be retrieved.

The bridge continued to the other side of the river, being less springy on the last two fifths of the way. The bank of the river was lower on that side. A walkway was constructed of wooden planks, built upon stilts and connected to the bridge. This was very sturdy. The river flooded out of banks after heavy periods of rain. The bank on the road side was high enough to contain the river on that side, however the water on the far side would flow onto flat ground and spread a long ways. The walkway was built so people could travel the bridge without getting in the floodwater.

The U. Z. Burnett kids, Pat, Bill, Judy and Becky had to walk across the swinging bridge to ride the school bus. The whole neighborhood crossed the bridge to get their mail until a rural route was established. Some folk crossed the bridge to walk to the Church.

Brave teenagers used the bridge for entertainment. They would run the entire length of the bridge causing the bridge to swing more than usual. Different people walking in both directions also caused the bridge to swing or sway more.

Standing on the bridge and looking into the swift river underneath was exciting also. Occasionally fish could be seen swimming in the water. During a very heavy storm the bridge was damaged and had to be replaced.

The bridge still stands today. It is still fun to cross the swinging bridge. I am always reminded of my childhood days.

THE SWIMMING HOLE

When we think of swimming today, we usually think of a pool with clear blue water. Not so back when we were growing up. We went swimming in the river, as did all others who swam. We lived right by the river for a few years. After we moved, we still walked to the river. At this time the river ran parallel to the road by our house. The house sat about thirty feet above the road. We would walk a ways (meaning a quarter of a mile or more. A good ways meant anywhere from a quarter of a mile to four or five miles. A good long ways meant even farther.) We would walk about one quarter of a mile to what was then called the Swimming Hole. It was a social gathering of all who liked to swim. The Swim Hole was actually a deep place in the river, nature made. The water was about eight to ten feet deep. My Daddy was a good swimmer. My brother Marvin and I could not swim. Daddy would carry one of us on his back through the swim hole to what was known as the sand bar. The sand bar was just that, sand not covered by water and a wonderful place to play. Daddy would instruct us not to move until he returned with the other kid. When both of us were safely deposited onto the sand Daddy would swim while we played in the sand. We knew not to get into the deep water, we did exactly as Daddy said. We loved to get to play in the river. I was very small. Mama was not a big fan of the water, so she stayed on the bank of the river and watched my brother Charles. Mama gave Daddy instructions to "watch the kids". Usually there were other women to talk with.

On a Sunday evening there might be fifteen to twenty people swimming. Some brought a quilt to stretch out in the shade and rest. We always had fun at the Swim Hole. Mama was always a little nervous as most mothers are, when we crossed the river on Daddy's back. Mama was always glad to get the family back home safely; I learned to love and respect the river.

The other swimming place was below the Hightower Church and was used for both swimming and baptising new converts and will be mentioned again in another story.

After we moved back to the old home place after building a new house, we still walked to the river to fish and swim. We moved to a different place a few years later, farther away from the river. We occasionally got to go back to the same old swim hole. At our new place we had a big creek to play in. We dammed up the creek, beavers would have been proud of us, and made a big swimming pond. We spent a lot of time in the creek. During the hot part of the day we were allowed to go to the pond. This was cherished time because there were so many chores to be done around the house and with the crops and farm animals.

I have always loved the river and actually any type of stream. I still like to wade and play in water.

SECTION TWO:
THE OLD HOME PLACE

MY ACCIDENT

For as far back as I can remember as a child, my Mother baked what was called sweet bread. She kept this bread in the cupboard up on the top shelf. My Daddy loved this bread. Mama packed it for his lunch when Daddy went to the woods to work. We kids liked the bread too.

One day Mama had been canning peaches. I was only about four years old at the time. Mama took the canner off the stove with the hot water still in the canner and sat it on the wooden floor where there was no rug. She never anticipated an accident happening. We had wood floors. The majority of the floor was covered with a lanoleum rug. About two feet around the edges were bare floor.

My older brother Marvin and cousin Emma and I were playing outside. We decided to come into the kitchen to get some sweetbread. Mama had gone out of the kitchen to cool off. She was canning on a wood-burning cook stove in the summer. The kitchen could get very hot. I climbed upon a chair to get to the cupboard. Marvin and Emma both climbed onto the same chair crowding me off. I fell with my left foot going into the scalding hot water. I was screaming, Mama came running to the kitchen. She grabbed me up and took off to the creek to stick my foot in some cold water. My Daddy had to walk about a mile down the road to Earnest Simonds store and get him to take me to the doctor. We seldom went to the doctor back then. My foot really hurt a lot. The doctor put some salve on the burn and wrapped the foot with white gauze. I could not walk on my sore foot. I had to be carried everywhere I went. My foot finally healed after about six weeks. Scars remain today on that foot. We still climbed onto the chair to reach the sweet bread, only one at a time. My mother never did set the canner on the floor to cool again.

DOLLS ON WHEELS

When I was very small or maybe before I was born, the state built a new road by our house. The new road replaces the curvy old road. The old road remained but was not used by vehicles as the two roads emerged together at places. I do not remember the construction of the new road. I was very familiar with the old road We used the old road to travel from our house up to Emma's house and visa versa.

Emma had several dolls. She would load them into a homemade wooden wagon and travel down the old road to our house. Aunt Edna would watch Emma until she was out of sight, at that time she would be in sight of our house. She would call out our names. If we were outside we heard her and went to meet her and the wagon of dolls. I only had one rag doll, after the demise of my rag doll I did not have any doll. I was always thankful to Emma for sharing her dolls with me.

If Aunt Edna did not come to visit with Em, she would write a note and say how long Em could stay at our house. Sometimes she would just say "I get to stay two hours." When the allotted time was up, we would load up the dolls into the wagon. Marvin and I would walk back up the old road with Emma to her house and stay for an appointed time. That was great fun.

Emma had a makeshift playhouse that was located on the side of their real house just underneath the kitchen window. One day we were playing out side. We would get red clay dirt from the road bank to make our mud pies. The dishes were cracked or chipped saucers and cups that were to bad for the real kitchen table. This particular day we had been playing for some time in the playhouse. All of a sudden out through the open kitchen window came a pan of dishwater. Aunt Edna must have forgotten where we were playing.

We started screaming and running toward the kitchen door with dirty dishwater dripping from our head and clothes. Aunt Edna felt kind of bad for messing us up. Our mud pies really were muddy, more so than intended. We got cleaned up and tried to salvage our mud pies. We finally just gave up and dumped them out. We were careful to let Aunt Edna know where we were playing after that. Aunt Edna would stick her head out the window and shout "you had better get out of the way. I am going to throw out the dishwater". There was no sink or running water in their house at that time.

Uncle Lloyd was a man who loved to play pranks on people. He had been over to see Calvin Wikle one evening and did not get back until after dark. Uncle thought he would scare us, (Aunt Edna, Emma and Me). He started making these funny noises and knocking on the window. Aunt Edna stopped what she was doing and listened. The noise continued, we could not figure out what was making the sound. My Aunt thought that her husband was the culprit. Aunt Edna goes into the bedroom and gets the loaded shotgun from its usual place and quietly makes her way into the kitchen. Again we heard the noise. Emma and I were right behind Aunt Edna. We were not about to be left in the other room with such spookiness going on.

Aunt Edna eased the kitchen window open, no light was on. She stuck the shot gun out the window and said "Lloyd is that you? if that is you, I will give you to the count of three to let yourself be known or I will commenced to shooting". Uncle Lloyd must have gotten scared; He knew Aunt Edna could shoot good. He started hollering in a very scared voice. "Edna don't shoot me this is Lloyd." She said "you had better get yourself in this house then." Uncle Lloyd came in through the front door very shortly. Aunt Edna said, "you had better not do that again, next time I will just start shooting". I really think my Uncle believed her.

My Uncle Lloyd never harmed anyone. When he had been nipping the whisky bottle a little too often He would come in and go to bed and sleep "it off ". Aunt Edna and Emma had come to our house this particular day. I went home with them as usual. When we got to the house the door was latched from the inside. We could not get into the house. It was decided that we would have to climb in at the bedroom window. I was elected to do just that. Uncle Lloyd's bed was directly below the window. I was encouraged to be careful and not disturb Uncle Lloyd. I carefully climb in at the window, all is going well until my shoe got caught on the window seal and I lost my grip when I yanked hard to loosen my shoe, with Emma and Aunt Edna pushing me. I fell in the window and landed right on top of my Uncle Lloyd's head. He came alive. He had no clue what was happening. He thought he had been attacked. He came up out of the bed with me on his head and crashed me to the floor. He started hollering, "what in the world are you doing?" I was laughing so hard that I could not answer him. I think he recognized me." He said, "what did you do that for." I said, "you locked the door and we couldn't get into the house".

When we got the door opened Aunt Edna told him to"leave the door open from now on."

I think he was glad to do just that. Every once in awhile he would say to me "don't you break in on me any more." I didn't.

I really did love my Uncle. I missed him so much after he died, and still do today.

FIRST GRADE

I started into first grade in the fall of 1954 at the Almond Elementary School. I was six and a half years old.

That same summer just a few weeks before school started, my mother was very sick. She had been diagnosed with Rheumatic Fever, untreated as a child. My mother was weak and hadn't been getting out much. My Aunt Edna came down the road by our house with her cow on a rope leash. The road banks were not mowed and the grass along side was great for the cows to eat. Most cows would follow along and not need much attention.

Aunt Edna asked Mama to come out with her while she grazed the cow. Mama walked a little ways and leaned against the bank. The bank was about eight feet high. The dog went up into the woods behind Mama. The dog must have scared a big black snake form its resting place. The snake came down the bank. Across my Mama's shoulders and into her lap. She took her hands and raked the snake

45

from her lap. The snake then wrapped around her legs. She passed out. My Aunt Edna came running and untangled the snake from my Mama's legs and started smacking my Mama in the face and calling her name. My Mama was very weak and we helped her back to the house. I was with my mama when this happened. I was scared to death. That night my Mama had a full-blown heart attack and when my Daddy got her to the hospital, the doctor gave her very little hope of recovering.

Dr. W. E. Mitchell told her that she would never sweep her floor again. Her heart was really damaged. My Mama stayed in the hospital for two weeks. After coming home, Mama was very sick. My Grandma took care of her and us kids. My Daddy was working every day, making about five dollars each day. Mama's medicine cost four dollars each day. That did not leave much money for any thing else. This went on for a couple of months. My Mama was improving a little.

We went to school barefooted as did a lot of the other kids. As the weather turned cold some of the kids started wearing shoes. I did not have any shoes to wear. As fall wore on the mornings were really cold. Frost was on the ground and I was still going to school without any shoes. I knew that my mama needed her medicine and I didn't really think about not having shoes .

One frosty morning when I got to my seat in Mrs. Helen Lovingood's class, there was a shoe box in my chair. I peeked inside. There was a beautiful pair of red tennis shoes. I knew they were not mine so I took them to the teacher's desk and asked her about them. She said," I guess they are yours, they were in your chair." I asked where they came from. Mrs. Lovingood said "I guess Santa Claus came to see you early." I asked why he didn't come to see every one else early. She said "I guess you needed shoes and no one else did." I put the shoes on my feet with her prodding. They were a perfect fit. I was so proud of those shoes. I made a vow in my heart that day to some day help people who were in need.

The shoes came right before Thanksgiving. My Mama had told us kids that we would not be getting any thing at Christmas, there just wasn't any money. We were not taught to believe in Santa Claus. On the Saturday before Christmas, a big ton truck pulled into our driveway; actually it was just a dirt road. People started getting out of the truck. We never had much company and of course we were curious. We were peeking out the windows. The people started taking boxes from the back of the truck and coming toward our house. We opened the door and they brought the boxes into the front room. They went back to the truck and made another trip, and another. The whole floor was full of boxes. Inside those boxes were groceries, and more groceries. I had never seen so many groceries. There were other boxes, and when the lid was opened we saw apples, oranges. Tangerines, nuts of all kinds, there was every kind of candy that could be thought of.

We kids were all excited, my Mama and Grandma was crying, Daddy didn't know what to do. The people were hugging everybody. My Mama had been working at the VanWrought Hosiery Mill before she got sick. The employees at the plant found out about Mama's condition and our situation, they opened up their hearts and pocketbooks and filled our home with much needed supplies. That's not all; each kid had a gift for Christmas. Mine was a Bible storybook. I was just learning to read at school. I read every page in the book many many times. I wore the pages out reading the book.

Again I vowed to help people when I got big and had the money. Christmas did come to our house that year. We had candy most of the winter. Mama hid part of it so we would not eat all of it in a few days. I have never forgotten the wonderful feeling of knowing people cared about us.

A few years ago I wrote Mrs. Lovingood a letter at Christmas time and thanked her for the shoes and told her of the mission work I am involved in today. She was thrilled with the letter. Mrs. Lovingood wrote me back and told me how the letter had brightened up her Christmas Holidays. Mrs. Lovingood you were a wonderful teacher.

SECTION THREE:
WIGGINS CREEK

LOOK OUT

We were always instructed by our parents and Grandma to "look out" for snakes. We grew up where snakes were plentiful. There were two poisonous snakes, the copperhead and the rattlesnake. Copperheads were more common to us than the rattlesnakes.

My cousin Maylee Sutton had been bitten by a rattlesnake at the age of five. We had heard the story over and over. Maylee got really sick and nearly died from the snakebite. My uncle Adam carried her on his back for several miles before catching a ride into town to see the doctor. Any time we were around Maylee, she gave us more instructions of being careful to "look out".

During 'DOG DAYS", which from Webster Dictionary states "being reckoned from the heliacal rising of the Dog Star Sirius", the period from early July to early September when the hot sultry weather of summer usually occurs in the Northern Hemisphere. 2 – A period of stagnation or inactivity.' There are controversy dates of dog days.

Some say forty days, others say six weeks. The dates have recently been changed again. Dog Days are the hot days of summer and snakes are crawling. The snakes also shed the skin during this time. When the scales are over the snake's eyes while shedding the skin, the snakes are blinded and strike at any movement or sound. We were constantly on the "look out".

My brother Charles grew cantaloupes and watermelon this particular summer. Every day he went to check on his melons. One day Charles found a big copperhead wrapped around one of the cantaloupes. That was a big surprise.

One summer one of our milk cows fell off the bank into a seep hole in the creek and broke her neck. We were saddened by this loss. The cow had to be buried. The whole family turned out to help burry the cow. I sat down on a rock to watch the digging of the grave. My Mama saw me and made me get up off the rock. She said,"There might be a snake under that rock." There was a slick place by the rock. Later when the cow had been buried and covered with dirt, big rocks were placed on top of the grave. When Daddy picked up the rock that I had been sitting on, with my feet dangling at the ground, there was a big copperhead.

My Grandma was in the barn putting the weeds (she had us kids pulling up) in for the cattle to eat. Grandma lit into hollering at us kids to bring her a hoe to kill the snake with. She usually carried a walking stick or hoe with her at all times just for that purpose. We took her the hoe and she killed the snake.

Several times we were greeted at the entrance of the root cellar by the familiar copperhead. Each time we were sent to the root cellar we were instructed to "look out" and rightly so. There were plenty of the creeping creatures.

We usually had at least one good snake killing dog. When we went to pick berries or apples we always took the dog or maybe I should say the dog always went with us. You could tell by the way a dog barked when there was a snake spotted. We would always go to the dog. The dog would circle around the snake slowly and all of a sudden he would make a dive at the snakes head. He would snatch that snake up and snap it into pieces literally. If the dog caught the snake too far back from the head the snake would bite the dog. This occasionally happened. The bitten site would start to swell at once. Mama gave the dog a bowl of raw egg mixed with cream or milk, cream was better. We sometimes had to hold the dog's mouth open and pour the mixture into his mouth. The more time elapsed between the bite and the remedy the longer the recovery time. The treatment was repeated several times in the next couple of days. Turpentine was applied at the bite site. The dog would be very sick for several days but I don't remember one dying.

One day the mail man started hollering from his vehicle for someone to bring something to kill the snake that had wrapped itself around the mailbox post. That was the only rattlesnake killed on our property. Where there is one there is probably more. We were on the "look out".

The creek that runs through the property just below the house is still a haven to snakes. Water snakes are plentiful. Copperheads are still living close by. My brother lives in a doublewide near the creek. Last year I nearly stepped on a copperhead in his yard. This summer 2004 a copperhead came to reside on his front porch, under a tool box.

The copperhead has very distinctive markings. The head can be from a dull orange brown to a bright copper depending on the season. Before shedding the skin the colors are darker and dull in appearance. One just recently shed will be a brighter color. A series of red brown or dark brown bands seem to appear on a tan to pinkish cooper background. A darker line separates the dark from the light areas. The king snake is often mistaken for a copperhead. The copperhead lives on small rodents and birds. A snake can go for days without food or water, and are more active at night. Copperheads move in a straight line, they do not zig zag back and forth like the Black snake does.

If someone is bitten by a poisonous snake immediate medical attention should be sought. The longer the delay the more serious and the longer the recovery time will be.

THE FORMICA MINE

About sixty years ago Formica was mined from the ground. Formica is a shiny silver metallic-like substance having iridescent and reflective properties. The material was soft and in layers that could be separated very easily.

By the time we had moved on Wiggins Creek the Formica mining was completed in the mine close to our new house. The empty mine was above our house across the road and up on a hill. The mine could not be seen from our house but voices of children playing could be heard. We were allowed to go there and play.

The Formica was beautiful. We collected fragments that were left behind by the miners. The fun part of the mine was the opportunity of adventures of which the mine held. There was a roadway cut through the mountain with steep embankments on each side. One side was on a slope of about 75 to 80 feet from top to bottom. The other side was a drop off of about 30 feet. We were not allowed to be on the drop off side. We were allowed to play on the slope. Red clay dirt became our closest companion. We made a slide on the slope by sliding down the embankment on our behinds with feet and legs held straight out in front of us. We were hoping to push the loose rocks with our feet before our behinds made direct contact with them. After several trips down, we had the slope pretty well packed down and ready for the action. The hill was too steep to climb back up so we went around a longer route but not as steep. We had a genuine slide, not the kind you see today on playgrounds, but to us it was the finest in the land.

We always wore our oldest raggedest clothes when playing in the mine. Fred Ammons ' boys came to the mine to play also as did other kids in the neighborhood. There were some danger zones in the old mine. We explored every nook and corner. We were told to keep away from certain areas when there was no adult along. The adults could arrive at any minute to check to see if we were abiding by their rules. The mine was such a fun place to play we did not want to loose our chance to play there so we pretty much did as we were told. If the boys went a little beyond the safe bounds there would be someone on the lookout for incoming adults. A certain word was hollered and by the time the adult arrived all was in proper order.

The slide was only one of the attractions of the old mine. The run off rainwater collected in the road, making great mud puddles. We would take a run ago and slid into the puddle, trying to see who could last the longest before sliding down on our rear. We were one more mess by the time we got to the house. One other fun thing was the country bricks left by the sunshine drying the puddles. The red clay dirt would crack into different size pieces of "bricks". The bricks would be between one half to one inch in depth. You could carefully lift the dry brick off the ground. The girls especially liked the bricks. We made little houses by stacking the bricks on top of each other. If we could find some mud we would put the mud between the bricks and leave to dry. We would make a whole little village. The boys loved to come chasing each other through our village and of course demolish the whole thing. Tag was one of their favorite things in the mine. The broken dirt bricks then became our weapons. A dirt fight was sure to follow the demolition. The bricks carried quiet a punch if the target was with-in close range. The bricks broke into several pieces with each throw therefore making the ammunition smaller with each throw, soon putting an end to the fight. We knew never to complain to our parents so the conflicts were worked out among the kids.

By the time we reached home we would be covered from head to toe with either mud or red clay dirt. We did not have a bathroom in our house or even running water part of the time. We had to clean up at the creek. We usually filled up the big washtub with water in the mornings and by evening the water would be nice for a bath. We did not get in the tub for a bath until the red clay dirt was washed off because every one had to use the same bath water.

Bonnie Lou Cochran

At the creek was what we called a waterspout. The waterspout was constructed of long boards nailed together at a 90% angle making a V. The trough was placed in the water on a little hill then turned out from the creek making the water about two feet from the ground. This was where we kids got cleaned up, also the men washed up before the meals. We also used the waterspout for washing vegetables, any big pots and canning containers. A bar of soap lived in a tree beside the waterspout. The water seemed ice cold because it was the run off from a spring up on top of the mountain,, not the spring where we got our drinking water. Years later the water from that spring was piped into the house. The spring now supplies water to three houses.

There is little trace of the Formica mine now. The trees are really large camouflaging the whole mine. The deep ravine still remains but has grown over with trees. The memories of the old mine return to me each time I see a piece of Formica or hear the mine mentioned.

MAKING BUTTER AND BUTTERMILK

I wrote this story as a single event to enter into a magazine contest. I want to leave it as it was presented, even though I have already mentioned some things that is covered in this story. This story was the beginning of what led to this book.

I grew up in the 50's and 60's on a farm in The Great Smoky Mountains of North Carolina. (Well I don't think you could really call it a farm), It was about 70 acres of mountains, with only about 4 acres of flat land, Our house, vegetable garden, potato patch, corn field, sweet potato patch and tobacco field along with the barn and pig lot took up the flat land, The pasture was the side of a large hill. We had free-range chickens for our egg supply and Sunday dinner, (chicken and dumplings). There were usually two milk cows, at least one, giving milk for our family, and sometimes a baby calf. We had a mother pig and lots of little pigs that found a new home after about 6 weeks. We had a fattening pig that was butchered in the fall.

There was never a dull moment around our house. There were many chores to be done. Our family of eight, and sometimes nine, depending on where my uncle was living at the time. My maternal grandmother along with my parents and all five of us children. We had to raise a lot of food to get us through the winter. Life was hard, but our house was filled with love. My Daddy cut cordwood and helped another uncle get out logs to sell, but there wasn't ever enough money. We always had enough food. We put up about 1000 quart jars of food each year, plus "salted down" the hog. We dried green beans, called leather britches, and dried corn to make hominy and corn meal.

Mama usually milked the cows, until my older brother took over this chore. We all had chores to do. From the milk, we had plenty of milk to drink; we had cream to make biscuits and all the wonderful things you can make from real cream. Mama would skim part of the cream from the milk and pour the cream into a 3-gallon crock churn jar. This crock was positioned beside the wood cook stove to stay warm and to sour the milk and cream that was added daily. When "just the right amount" was in the jar and it was "sour enough" we had to churn. Mama would take the white flour sackcloth from the top of the crock and add the dasher and lid to the crock. To churn, one had to lift the dasher up and down about a thousand times, and this chore usually was mine, being the oldest girl. It took a long time to complete the churning, my arms would ache. I would change hands often. When little specks of bright yellow clumps started sticking to the dasher, I would be so thankful, because that meant before long butter would be made. I tried to go fast like I had seen Mama and Grandma do, but it just was not possible. I would ask, is it butter yet? Mama would say, "just keep churning" After a while longer bigger clumps of yellow would be visible on the dasher. Mama would say, "just keep churning". I did. Finally, Mama would take the dasher and finish the churning. When the lid was removed there would be big clouds of bright yellow butter, all the butter was dipped off the top and this left what was called butter milk. I always wondered why it wasn't called butter less milk. We loved to eat the fluffy butter on top of hot berry cobbler, hot bread, or mashed potatoes. Most of the butter was placed into a butter mold. This was a wooden cup with a handle in the bottom connected to a removable part that had a carved flower or other design. The butter was patted firmly into the mold, making sure to get all the milk and air bubbles out. Then the handle was pushed and out came a beautiful half-pound of butter, with the flower showing on top. Some times this butter was sold, and some times we used it for company. Butter making was definitely an art.

Buttermilk was a stable drink that lasted for several days, the longer it "kept" the sourer it became. Some people liked it really sour, while others preferred it "mild". Both my Mother and my Grandma were noted for making good buttermilk, as well as being good cooks. You cannot buy that kind of buttermilk or butter in the grocery store. I crave good homemade butter and butter milk now.

On the wall of my country kitchen, I have the old dasher supporting an ivy vine. The mold sits proudly on a shelf, waiting to tell the story of "just keep on churning".

PAPER DOLLS

Back in the 50's growing up money was scarce. There never seemed enough to make ends meet, much less have any money for toys. Even at Christmas, we usually got clothes or shoes. We had to make our own toys or make-believe toys, or maybe one of our parents made a toy for us.

Long before Barbie and Ken became common house hold names, the Sears and Roebuck catalogue came to our rescue. In the catalogue were many nice dolls and toys for sale. We did not buy any of the toys. The catalogue itself was our prized possession; our new neighbors were Vance and Violet Winchester. The couple had three girls. The oldest was named Cathy, next was Sandy and Arlene. We became fast friends even though I was a couple of years older than Cathy. We played good together. Arlene was more my younger sisters Linda and Dianne's ages. She easily fit in with the older girl s also. The Winchester Girls were very talented with a pair of scissors and paste glue.

When their parents received a new Sears catalogue in the mail we were given the old one. The extra large catalogue held many treasures, (of course unseen by the natural eye of today.) The Winchester Girls taught me the fine art of cutting paper dolls from the catalogue. We all pilled up on the floor with the catalogue spread out before us. I don't ever remember us quarreling over who choose what. We took turns choosing our family as the pages were turned. We each wanted a nice looking family. After Dad, Mom, and the number of children we wanted, were determined, we carefully tore out the pages as we made our decisions. This was half the fun.

Each paper doll was carefully cut from the page and glued to a piece of cardboard. We also made a stand for each one by cutting a slit in a small straight piece of cardboard and connected it to the doll. This took at least one day of playtime. We had to wait for the glue to dry.

Next day our dolls could be moved in their upright position at our will. We cut a wardrobe for each one making extra tabs to attach the clothing to the dolls just the same as store bought paper dolls. Many times we had to revise and remodel with a bit of creativity to achieve a perfect or near perfect fit.

My friends lived in a big old farmhouse with a huge attic, where we could play and leave our doll family out to live their own "lives" when we were not present with them. We named each one a first, middle and last name. The last name being the same as ours or that of a cute boy we liked at the time. During the summer, rainy days were the best times to play as there were numerous farm chores to be done each day. Rainy days meant no working in the garden or fields. A very much-welcomed break.

Wintertime held more promise of time to spend with our doll family. We needed to make warm clothing for them anyway. We never tired of our paper dolls.

Violet was a mother to me, she just set another plate at the table, no questions asked. I felt so at home and so nurtured by her. Vance was really nice to me too. Their home was so comfortable, love abound.

After several years, my friends moved to Cashiers, N.C. It wasn't really far away but to us it was a world apart. They took their dolls with them and I was left with my own. Paper dolls never were as much fun again. Of course I missed my good friends terribly, and I missed Violet and Vance too.

Now I am a grand mother, and all through the years when I would get a Sears catalogue in the mail I would be immediately reminded of our childhood days and paper dolls. I have given my granddaughter a pair of scissors and a catalogue (no more Sears catalogues available). They enjoy cutting flowers and animals from the book, but modern toys have taken over at least half of their rooms and there is no thrill in creating a family of paper dolls cut from a catalogue.

I have kept in touch with my friends over the years and we occasionally see each other. The memories have kept us close at heart and it is fun to recall those good times of long ago

MY BABY DOLLS

When I was very young I remember having a rag doll. The doll did not have a special name. She was just "My Doll". I played with her all the time. I guess my Grandma had made the doll for me. My rag doll met with a disaster one day and the result was rag doll premature demise. I was very sad. My Daddy promised to buy me a new doll when he got the money. I knew money was scarce and it might be a long time before I would get a new doll.

Some time later, my Daddy came home with a big long brown box. We were all anxious to find out what was in the box. We were guessing everything. Finally Daddy opened up the box and brought out the most beautiful doll I had ever seen. The doll wasn't a baby doll, she was a little girl doll. The name on the box was Susie. My Daddy placed Susie Doll into my arms and said "this is the doll I promised you" I could not believe she was really mine. I saw the price tag on the box and I knew that my Daddy had made a big sacrifice for me. I was laughing and crying both at the same time. I fell in love with Susie Doll at first sight. I could tell that my Daddy was so proud of the new doll. Susie was dressed in a red and white blouse and a navy skirt. She was a rubber doll and would not break or fall apart.

Susie and I spent many many happy hours together. Every where I went so did my doll. The next year my baby sister Dianne was born. I loved her at first sight too. I was seven and a half years old. We became fast friends. As Annie (that's what we called Dianne) grew, she took first place in my heart. Susie was still a wonderful doll, but Annie was a live doll. I carried her around with me everywhere I went. It was a big help to my Mama for me to occupy my baby sister. Annie started calling me "Mama Bunt" (using my childhood nickname. I never did like that nickname, Marvin could not say Bonnie Lou when I was first born. He called me" Buntie" and the name stuck. I finally refused to answer to any thing other than Bonnie.) As Annie got older we dropped ie and just called her Ann. We still do.

All three of us girls played with Susie Doll. Actually we wore the poor thing "plumb out". That was the only doll I ever owned (after the rag doll), until many years later when I started collecting dolls as an adult.

My Uncle Lloyd Sutton never quit calling me by my nick name. He called me "Blunt" and always said it sort of drawn out. My Uncle

Everett Wikle called me Bunt. I loved both my Uncles so much. I really did not mind what they called me. My uncle Lloyd died at age 53 unexpectedly, a tragic loss to his family and mine.

SECTION FOUR: SPRING

SPRING CLEANING THE YARD

For most families spring-cleaning means cleaning the house from top to bottom. Back in the 50's growing up, spring-cleaning took on a different meaning. My Grandma volunteered to over see the task of spring-cleaning. She said, "If the yard ain't clean, the house ain't clean." The winters wind had left relics of broken twigs, dead leaves, all sorts of wood chips blown from the woodpile. The woodpile was the place where all wood was prepared. "Fire wood" for heating the house and the "stove wood" which was used in the wood burning cook stove in the kitchen. A large amount of wood was needed each winter to accommodate the two stoves. The meals and canning required "stove wood" all year long. The dogs had their secret hiding places for items, which were only of interest to dogs. A few pieces of broken pottery and a variety of other things lay dormant in the yard just waiting to be put out of their misery. Grandma was happy to oblige.

Clad in our oldest old clothes and worn gloves, carrying shovel, rake, hoe and broom. Yes broom and tow sack. We commenced the task. First we all were assigned a section of the yard to scour for any of the items previously listed above and any other items found that are not listed above. We each carried a one gallon tin bucket with no handle to collect the trash. When the bucket was full or an item found that was too large for the bucket, off to the tow sack we went. Every corner and cranny had to be explored and left free of debris. Next came Grandma's demanding questions, "Did you get by the corner of the house? Did you go by the garden fence? Did you go behind the house? Don't forget the outhouse." One more swipe was made; once again we dumped our loot into the now bulging tow sack.

My oldest brother, Marvin was considered the most mature kid (not the thoughts of every one, myself included, but agreed upon by all the adults and of course Marvin) Any way Marvin was given the honor of using the yard rake, well it really wasn't a yard rake, but a garden rake. In those days, one used and made do with what you had on hand. Marvin started raking the yard collecting anything that was left from the scavenger hunt. He would proudly call for the findings to be picked up in the shovel. (We never knew what a dust pan was, we used a flat piece of heavy paper inside the house to retrieve the dirt from the floor after sweeping) Each morsel had to be gotten up and discarded into the tow sack. Another sack was fetched from the back porch where several sacks awaited their turn of rightful use.

My younger brother, Charles and I had heated discussions on who was suppost to do what. I usually won out and got my way because Charles had a calm manner and the patients of Job. I was usually the one carrying on the heated discussion. I would hold the shovel and He would pick up the morsel found. The hoe was used to up root any sharp rock peeking its head out of the ground.

Now a days we would think the lawn mower would have made an appearance. Well back in the 50's we had never even seen a lawn mower, except the push mower our elderly neighbor Mr. Mose Wikle owned. I'm not talking about a motor powered mower. I am talking about a big handle connected to a large round contraption with two wheels. The blades were confined inside the round contraption. When you pushed on the mower the wheels turned and the blades turned also cutting the grass. At least that was the intended use. When I tried to mow with the mower, I could not push the thing through the tall grass fast enough to cut the grass, instead it looked as though something had been chewing on the tips of the grass and kindly squished the grass into a state of pure ugliness. Needless to say it took some doing to get the grass back into presentable shape before the neighbor spotted the dilemma. My mature older brother came to my rescue. (Well maybe I did think he was more mature, just that one time.) We did not own any such mower.

We really did not need a lawn mower anyway. Several reasons for that. We had free-range chickens, (partly the reason a shovel was needed previously.) The chickens scratched up any grass before it had a chance to grow to any size. There were five kids in our family, along with our parents and maternal grandmother, plus 2or 3 dogs and at least one good cat trampling on the grass. If this wasn't enough to keep down grass we had a milk cow hobbled. Hobbled means tied with a rope (made into a bridle) about her head and the other end of the rope tied to a stob (stake) in the ground. Thus the bovine would nibble any grass in her path. Sometimes a kid would be holding the other end of the rope, allowing her to graze at will, she would see one blade of grass in the yard and go for it with little or no resistance from the kid. Occasionally she would leave behind a pile of stuff that would have to be removed with the shovel. I gladly consented to my older brother as being the most mature kid and given the honor of using the shovel or was more than willing to allow my younger brother the privilege to maneuver the shovel.

If all above was not enough to keep down any thriving efforts of the green stuff, my Grandma would get us kids out early in the morning to pull weeds and grass to feed the fattening hog. Thus leaving only bare ground for the yard.

Any way it was time to finish tidying up the yard. The next item of use was the broom (yes the broom). Grandma preferred to navigate the handle of the broom all by her self. She was the best sweeper of all. The broom served two fold. If any of us kids were goofing off or standing idle, she could reach across the yard with her hand connected to the broom handle and whack us right on the rear. Quickly drawn to attention we asked what else needed to be attended to and swiftly proceeded to please Grandma

When all the trash had been carried and placed on the already big pile to be burned on a calm damp day, and Grandma put up the broom the yard shined almost as bright as her beautiful blue eyes. Job well done, next we would start inside the house.

HOME MADE WAX ROSES

Several weeks before Decoration Day or what is now Memorial Day, my mother and grandma, we always called her Maw, would begin making crepe paper flowers to adorn the graves of their loved ones. After seeing mama and Maw's beautiful flowers, our elderly widowed neighbor, Mose Wikle asked them to make flowers for him to put on his departed dear wife's grave. Most people could not afford to buy store bought flowers then. The flowers sold by the stores were not the beautiful ones available today. They were hard plastic, which soon faded from the hot sun. Mr. Wikle would buy enough supplies, which included crepe paper of all colors, wire for the stems and paraffin wax to dip the flowers into to make them stronger, to make twice what he wanted. He got half and we got the other half. Sometimes Mama and Grandma would buy more supplies; there were many relatives who had already departed from this world.

Roses were the most favored and actually the easiest to make. To make a rose, a wire about eight inches would be cut, or the desired length for the stem. My daddy would always join in the fun by being the official wire cutter. He would cut all the wire needed to make all of the flowers, which would be about twenty dozen flowers. Mama or Maw would cut a pattern or find last years patterns, made from a stiff sheet of paper or cardboard. Each size petal and leaf had a pattern. Depending on the mood of Mama and Maw or the request of Mr. Wikle would determine just how many of what type flowers they would make. Any budding flower makers were encouraged to participate in the project. This was a necessary task, even though it was a fun thing, it got "old" long before they were completed. I wanted to try my hand at rose making, under the watchful eye of my instructor Mama.

The center of the flower was a 2x3 inch piece of yellow crepe paper with a slit cut every 1/8 of an inch along the 3-inch side, leaving ½ inch intact, thus resembling a comb. After cutting the wire daddy would make a loop on one end with the pliers. The yellow center was connected to the loop and held.

The petals were cut from the crepe paper in the shape of a dogwood leaf with a rounded upper edge instead of the point. The outer edge was scraped with one blade of the scissors to create a curled look like that of a real rose petal. The thumbs were placed in the middle of the petal and pushed in opposite directions, slowly, creating a puffed area. Several were fixed before assembly began.

With the wire already holding the yellow center in hand, place a puffed petal around the center and continuing to hold tight add two more petals. The center should be completely surrounded by now. Holding tight enough was the hardest problem. Four more petals were added, surrounding the first three. Two more rounds of four petals were then added, making sure to cover the in-between spaces of the previous round of petals. Two leaves cut from the green crepe paper in the shape of the Dogwood leaf was placed opposite each other on the wire at the bottom of the rose. Hold tightly! A thin strip of green crepe paper, which was cut in advance (now can be bought at the store, called florist tape) was wound around the base of the flower and slightly stretched as it was wound. Continue winding the green down the stem until it is completely covered. The end was twisted off at the bottom. One flower completed. I'm not sure rose would be the proper name for my flower, it resembled something like a wind blown, over mature rose with drooping petals and wilted leaves. Mama helped me tighten the petals and I had passed the first lesson in rose making. Mama and Maw had already made half dozen beautiful roses each. Nineteen dozen more to go. Soon I had mastered the fine art of rose making, or so I thought. I was so proud!! My roses were nowhere as nice looking as the ones of my talented adult peers. My roses were at least acceptable for Mama's use. The rose making continued for many days, some days being more productive than others, due in part to the many chores of farm life. The garden had to be planted and attended to, as well as the other regular household chores.

When the twenty dozen flowers were completed, there were red, yellow, pink, and white roses, along with the same color of carnations. Mr. Wikle liked a special flower called hyacinth, which was very difficult to make. This flower was made from pink, purple or blue crepe paper. I never did learn to make that flower.

Carnations were made by fan folding six to eight layers of square sheets of the crepe paper. (The squares need to be twice the size of the finished flower. 8" squares make 4" flowers.) Twist a wire around the center and fan out the paper. Starting at the top sheet gently separate the papers to give a full blossom look. Add a leaf and roll with green strip of crepe paper. To make "mums" or Chrysanthemum, use scissors to cut the carnation petals into narrow strips after the flower is completed. Kleenex tissue makes pretty paper flowers also. Spray a "dab" of perfume on the tissue flower and wear in hair or as a corsage.

In a large pot on the backside of the wood-burning cook stove, several blocks of paraffin wax had melted and stood ready for duty, the dipping pot. The wax was needed to add to the life of the crepe paper flowers. The first rain would deal a fatal blow to the flowers if they had not been dipped into the wax. Mama would hold a flower in her right hand, turn it upside down and with the dipping pot pulled close to the edge of the stove, she gently and swiftly immersed the willing flower into the hot wax. Immediately she brought the flower back up out of the wax. The now dripping flower was held over the pot until every last drop of excess wax had dripped back into the pot. Not a single drop was wasted. After all there were lots more flowers to be dipped. Mama would turn the flower back to its upright position and place it into the side of a cardboard box with a corrugated edge. Flowers were placed at intervals along the box edge, so as not to allow the box to become over balanced and topple over, ruining the beautiful flowers.

Occasionally mama would stop and take a break from the hot dipping task. I begged to be allowed the honor of waxing a flower. Mama finally relented and gave me intense instructions of flower dipping. I was cautioned to be very careful, as the wax was hot and serious burns could result from improper respect to the wax. I proudly selected a rose I had made with my own two hands. I had carefully kept my roses separate from the others, with Mama's un-hesitated consent. If I do say so myself, my rose had character. I climbed upon a stool, rose in hand, I made the big plunge. I did not only submerge the poor thing, it met head –on with the bottom of the pot before I could retrieve it. My beautiful rose took on a whole new personality. The petals were squished flat. The rose looked as though it had been traveling at a high rate of speed before colliding with a brick wall. Mama did not laugh; I don't know how she kept from it. I cried "oh no, what happened to my rose"?

Mama said, "Honey it will be okay. We will use it as filler." She didn't even call it a flower, only "it". I knew the ugliest flowers were used as filler, put into the middle of the bunch to take up space. The prettier flowers were used on the outside of the bunch or as a single flower. Several more deformed fillers came out of the dipping pot before I mastered the art of wax dipping. Actually I probably was the only one to think I had the art mastered. Mama just said, "It takes time". I wonder what she meant by that statement.

A few days before Decoration Day, Mr. Wikle came to choose his flowers. Mama always allowed him first choice. I again had kept my flowers separate from the others. I watched cautiously while the flowers were chosen. I was hoping Mr. Wikle would not choose any of my creations. I was so pleased to find every single one of my prized poises still remaining in their rightful positions after his chosen flowers were taken away.

Come Sunday morning, we proudly began our journey to the Cemetery, each carrying a large box of beautiful hand made wax flowers. My Mama and Maw were known as talented flower makers. I noticed a few second glances from some of the women as we carefully placed our flowers onto the graves. I heard Mama say, "It was her first time making flowers. I think she will be good at it." Now what did she mean by that? There were many hand made flowers adorning the graves. None compared to the ones made by my Mama and Grandmother, unless of course those made by my

Aunt Edna. She also was a known talented flower maker. She and Mama were taught by Maw.

The flower making continued in the same fashion for several years. I did get better at making the flowers, I really did.

Now homemade wax flowers are a thing of the past, a dying art. The long rolls of crepe paper are not easy to find these days. However I did make some wax roses to put into fire started baskets last Christmas. My grandson David said, "Grandma you are really good at making flowers... I will have to tell my Mama, she will be so proud!

CORN FIELD RELAY

There were several reasons to grow corn. The corn was used to feed the cows, chicken, and hogs. The corn was also used to provide food for our family. We had creamed corn, which was the first use of the ear of corn. The corn was shucked and silks removed before bringing it into the house. Next the corn was washed and with a very sharp thin knife the tops of the kernel were clipped off inside a large bowl. The ear of corn was then scrapped, getting all the pulp from the cob. This was placed into a large pot and simmered on the stove. Since this was early corn and not fully mature there was more liquid in the corn making it thinner than desired. A half-cup of heavy cream with two tablespoons of flour mixed in and stirred until no lumps remained, was stirred into the corn. One teaspoon of salt was added per quart of corn. The corn continued to cook until done; this was served with hot biscuits. I have seen my Mama cook creamed corn in a dishpan she would be cooking for so many.

The corn was boiled on the cob when the kernels were full. My Grandma then sliced the kernels off with a sharp knife and made whole kernel corn. The corn could be eaten either way, also could be pickled either way. The corn was placed in a five gallon crock with salted water poured over the corn, A china plate and a heavy rock was placed over the corn to hold the corn in the liquid. A white flour sack was placed over the jar and tied. The corn was left to sour.

As the corn matured, just slightly firmer than boiling stage, we would grit the corn to make gritted bread. The gritter was hand made by my Daddy. He took a piece of stainless steel sheeting ten inches wide and eighteen inches long and drove nails through it. He removed the nails and continued to cover about three forth of the sheeting with the nail holes, which was done in the center. Using a one-inch by five-inch board two foot long, he curved the metal to make a dome attached it to the board with the jagged edge out, starting at two inches from the bottom of the board. The corn gritter was washed and ready to use. The corn was pushed over the jagged areas left by the nails. The corn fell into a bowl placed under the gritter. The gritted corn was made into bread. Two cups of gritted corn, ½ tsp baking soda, 1 tsp. salt, 1 tsp baking powder. One-cup buttermilk, stirred together and poured into a buttered hot cast iron skillet and cooked in a hot oven until golden brown. Eat with a meal or as a meal with lots of butter and sweet or buttermilk.

Another way to use corn that was too firm to cut off was to roast the corn on cob. There are several ways to do this. Pull the shuck back a couple of inches cut the tip off removing the silks, replace the shuck. Place ears of corn in hot oven and bake until the steam has stopped. The shucked and silked corn can be placed in a hot oven on the rack and baked until brown, or the corn can be wrapped in tin foil and baked. The corn wrapped in foil or kept in the shuck can also be buried in hot ashes and cooked. This is a good way to cook corn at a campfire. Corn may be roasted on the grill any of these ways.

The hominy was made from mature dry corn as well as the corn meal for corn bread. Hominy making will be described in a later story as it takes much work to make.

The mature dry corn could also be parched by placing one cup of kernels in a skillet generously coated with bacon grease. Cook several minutes until browned.

There were always eight of us to feed, and a lot more on Sunday after Church. We used a lot of corn. A very large field was grown each year as well as sweet corn planted in the garden. We also planted our own popcorn.

The corn was usually planted after the ground was warm and no frost feared. The field had been plowed and harrowed now known as rotavated. After the ground was prepared it was "laid off" with a single foot plow. The corn grains were planted two or three to the "hill" usually done by my Mama if she was feeling well. We kids covered the corn.

The corn hoeing came next. My Daddy bartered with my uncle Lloyd, He would do our plowing for planting and hoeing and we would help him with his planting and hoeing. There were three of us kid s old enough to hoe; He had one daughter, Emma. Lloyd was my Daddy's younger brother, who was married to my Mama's sister Edna. We are double first cousins to Emma. (And later in life they had another daughter named Kimberly), but now Emma was an only child.

We usually hoed their corn first because Uncle Lloyd had the horse at his house. We got up early; Mama cooked a big breakfast for us to eat. We then, with hoes in hand walked through the woods on a walking trail that was used often by both families to go to and from each other's house.

By the time we arrived at their house, my uncle Lloyd would have fed and harnessed the horse, ready to begin plowing. My aunt Edna would have cooked breakfast and completed the morning chores, which included milking the cows and putting the milk in the spring box. Emma would have the dishes done. As my aunt cooked breakfast she would cook an extra pan of batter bread and a pan of corn bread. A big pot of pinto beans would be simmering on the back of the wood cook stove.

My uncle would start the plowing, Gee meant for the horse to go right. Haw meant for him to go left. Whoa meant for him to stop. Gitty up meant to go forward, Back was to back up. Gee haw meant to slow down and go to the right and so forth. The horse knew exactly what each word meant, but sometimes he would refuse to abide. That's when my Uncle would add a few unforbidden words for us kids to repeat, to the horses command. I'm not sure if the horse knew what they meant or not., but He usually "straightened right up". It could have been the tone of voice used by my uncle.

My Aunt would don her sun hat and grab her hoe as would the rest of us and into the cornfield we went. We knew if we hoed real fast and got finished early, we would be allowed to walk to the Baptising Hole below the Hightower Baptist Church and go swimming. The pond was also considered a community "swim hole".

By now Uncle Lloyd was three or four rows ahead with the plowing. We spread out, three to a row. One started on each end and one about one third way from the front and we hoed until we met the other person or we came to where someone had already hoed, then we moved to the next row and went back the way we came. This continued on until it was time for my Aunt to go to the house and complete the dinner. One of the best hoers were out, we had to take up the slack, which meant faster hoeing. We also had to "thin" the corn which meant we pulled out the smaller stalk if more than two were in a "hill".

We knew better than to cover up any weeds with dirt, if caught we would have to re do the row.

We hoed as fast as we could trying so hard to keep up with the plowing. A bucket of cold water sat in the shade of a big apple tree in the middle of the field. There was a dipper in the water for us to drink from. Every one used the same dipper, gave it no thought.

It was soon time to stop to eat, we were so glad. The horse was probably glad for a rest too.

My aunt had boiled potatoes, turnip greens, deviled eggs, pickled cucumber chunks to go with the pinto beans and bread. There was a lot of fresh cows milk to drink. Buttermilk for the men and sweet milk for every one else. The men usually preferred the buttermilk. To end the meal was usually home canned peaches and applesauce. Butter, honey and molasses were always available. After the meal we would help with the dishes and be allowed to rest "a little while" during the hottest part of the day. Soon we were back to the toil. It was hotter and we were full, so hoeing slowed a little. We would have to remind each other about the swimming afterwards. We did not know how to swim, we called playing in the water "swimming". The cool waters of Lick Log Creek sure felt good after a day of hoeing corn. We usually didn't take extra clothes to swim in, we didn't have a bathing suit any way. We just swam in our shorts and shirts we were wearing. We were usually barefoot. We just wore the wet clothes back home and by the time we walked home the clothes were dry and caked with dirt.

We went to bed tired that night and prayed for rain so we could rest a few days before hoeing our corn field.

BABY CHICKENS

Back in the 50's jobs were scarce. My favorite aunt and uncle was Lloyd and Edna Sutton, their daughter, my cousin Emma was my double first cousin. I stayed at their house almost as much as I stayed at my own. I was one of five children and Emma was an only child. My aunt and uncle decided to go into the chicken business, raising chickens and selling their eggs. Up went a really large chicken house. Long rows of screened wire covered the open window spaces. The air could circulate nicely through the entire house. The building was divided, one very large area, a smaller area and another area was used to store the chicken feed. In the large area water troughs were installed along with feeders. The feeders being containers with cut outs in the bottoms where chickens could stick their heads in and eat until the heart was content or tummy full or another chicken moved one out and took the position at the dinner table.

The small area was the first place you came into when entering the chicken house. A bed and a few other necessary items were here. You guessed it; we were going to sleep with the chickens.

Finally the much-anticipated day arrived. A big delivery truck stopped at my uncle's house. The driver asked if this was where the owners of thousands of new born baby chicks lived, Assuring him that they were the rightful owners, he was pointed in the direction of the bright new chicken house. There were boxes and boxes and more boxes of tiny little heads peaking out the side just waiting to find their new home. Each little one-day-old chick looked like a tiny ball of bright yellow fuzz. The sounds coming out of their mouths were new sounds to us, but probably the perfect sound for frightened baby chicks. Each chick was carefully hand lifted out of the crate and counted as she (she being the sex of 90% or more of the chicks ordered) was placed onto the ground, which was covered with new, sweet smelling wood shavings. The male chicks were crated separately. After all the chicks were safely placed in their new home the deliveryman went on his way. The chicks had to have close observation and scattered about often to keep them from getting in a big huddle, causing some to be trampled to death.

We made our bed in the chicken house clad with flashlights, lanterns, water and snacks to aid in our survival during the night. My aunt and uncle took turns watching the tiny babes during the night. My cousin and I enjoyed the excitement of a campout. This continued for several days. I did not have the privilege of enjoying every night of sleeping in the chicken house, but the nights I was there were very much enjoyed.

Almost daily you see a change in the young chicks. Within a few weeks their golden feathers had turned snow white. The sound coming from them changed as much as the feathers had. The sleeping quarters were moved back into the house. More and more feed was delivered by the delivery truck.

The chickens were devouring the food. It was so much fun to watch them drink water. They would stick their heads into the water and then raise their head high in the air to swallow and repeat the process again and again.

After what seemed forever, the big day finally came when a snow-white egg was spotted on the ground. Nesting boxes were positioned along the walls, several in a row, with repeated rows three or four high. The chickens had been moved into larger areas as they grew. The new layers did not immediately use the boxes for laying their eggs. The eggs were dropped on the ground. We had to be very careful where we walked to prevent breakage of the precious eggs. The eggs were collected into a large wire basket every few hours during the day. The most eggs were picked up in the morning although the hens did lay all during the day. Each hen would lay one egg per day, occasionally skipping a day. The eggs were carried to the root cellar by one of the adults. The root cellar was a cool place to keep the eggs as well as a comfortable cool place to clean and sort the eggs. Each egg was carefully examined for any cracks; the cracked eggs were used by the family and shared with other family. A bowl of water with a few drops of bleach added was placed near each person and a cloth was dipped into the water and squeezed. The damp cloth was used to wipe each egg. If an egg looked small it was weighed on a tiny scale. There was a bowl used for culls. Any double yolks were set aside separately. The eggs went into a large crate. It took hundreds of eggs to fill one crate. The same deliveryman took the eggs in the truck, after leaving the feed and groceries.

The most interesting part was the fact that no money was given to the deliveryman. No money was given to my aunt. She just signed her name onto a ticket. After several months (or maybe sooner) my aunt finally got a check for the eggs. Up until that time it took all the eggs to pay for the feed and groceries. From then on a check came each time the truck came.

As time went on, new baby chicks arrived again and again. The older chickens were also sold making room for new layers. Each new shipment was given the same tender loving care as the first ones.

Needless to say there were always plenty of eggs for all needs. We ate them boiled, fried, scrambled. Eggs were used in cooking many dishes. Eggs were pickled in a large jar. There were eggs, eggs, and more eggs. My aunt and uncle continued to raise chickens for several years.

EASTER SUNDAY

My Aunt Edna always has had a knack for making pretty things. Including cakes, candy, crafts and sewing. She could whip up a batch of candy in a very short time. The day before Easter was one of those times. She made pastel centers dipped in chocolate or other candy coating. She allowed us to help her roll the candy into balls. She would flatten them and dip in the coating. These were a real treat. She had to hide some for Uncle Lloyd and to keep for the next day. We loved the candy and sampled every piece that we could get by with.

On Easter Sunday afternoon we would all get together and go on a picnic. We usually went up on the river someplace. The Grownups would hide the colored eggs for us. A lot of people have commented on there not being any Christian meaning in the hiding of the eggs. I strongly disagree. The colored eggs represented the many different races of people. God is not partial to the different color of peoples skin. We were not partial to the color of the eggshell either. Placing the eggs into the grass or hiding place, represented the burial of Jesus. Finding and bringing the eggs from hiding represented the resurrection of our Lord and Savior Jesus Christ. Easter is all about Jesus.

The Easter Bunny was not a part of our celebrating the holiday. We knew nothing about the bunny, except what we learned at school. He never brought any baskets of candy to our house. Aunt Edna made the candy. We made our own Easter baskets from the large oatmeal boxes, saved through the year. The top was cut off and we covered the box with scrapes of crepe paper, saved from the flower making paper the year before. We added buttons; pieces of lace and what ever other scrap that could be used to embellish the box. We were very proud of our baskets.

The Easter eggs were dyed using food coloring, warm water and a little vinegar. I have often used that method of dyeing eggs even recently, with the commercial dyes more available now than back then. There is a pride with in us when our own hands have created things from recyclables. (Boy did we recycle when I was growing up?)

After we moved to Wiggins Creek, my Daddy traded for an old junker car. He did not have any driver's license but he would drive us around on the back roads. We would load the food and colored eggs in their homemade baskets and go. It was amazing how many people could ride in one car. The back seat held unlimited space. We have packed as many as a dozen people in one vehicle.

We ate food brought, which was usually fried chicken and potato salad. The eggs were hidden and hunted. The grownups would sit and talk. We kids took turns hiding the eggs over and over until it was time to go home. We usually ate the eggs that were colored all during the day. We had a contest to see who could eat the most eggs.

At supper this particular Easter Sunday, Daddy was one egg behind me. I thought I had won the contest. My Daddy decided he wanted another couple of eggs cooked. He told me to fry him two eggs and put a lot of black pepper on them. I was reluctant, but I put the eggs on to cook. When I reached for the black pepper, I saw all Mama's spices there together on the warmer shelf of the wood cook stove. A clever idea came to my mind. I reached for the all spice, the darker of the spices. It kind of resembled black pepper. I really piled it on. I put the eggs before my Daddy and took my place at the table. Daddy bit into the eggs a large fork full. In just an instant he started gagging and carrying on. I made my big mistake here. I could have gotten by with the spice as a mistake if I had not laughed. I got so tickled at him. I started laughing so hard. No one else knew what was going on. My Daddy ran outside and started throwing up. I was still laughing. When he came back into the kitchen, he was not laughing. He was so angry. That was one of the two times that my Daddy whipped me.

Eating Easter eggs never was a contest again. Even if I did get a spanking I still thought it was funny. I have laughed every time I have thought of the trick since. Even today, while I am writing this, I have to laugh. My Daddy is no longer with us, I miss him so much. Every time that I ever mentioned spicing his eggs, I have laughed. Daddy would always say "yeah and you got your butt beat too" The other time that I got a whipping from my Daddy was when I was about sixteen years old and sassed my Mama. That was not funny.

SECTION FIVE: SUMMER

THE WILD BLACKBERRY PATCH

The wild blackberry is a sure sign of Country. The berries start to ripen by the first of July. First they are red but red is not ripe, and are very sour in this stage. When the berry is completely black it is ripe. My Mother loved blackberries and used them in a variety of recipes. We had canned blackberries, which were used in cobblers and pies during the winter. The berries could be eaten right from the jar as a snack, the berries could be strained of the juice and the juice drank as a remedy for several stomach ailments. Blackberry juice would "stay on the stomach" when nothing else would. Blackberries should be used or "put up" right away as they will not keep long off the vine. The juice will start to bleed from the berry and loose some of its good qualities. Blackberries are very delicate and require a minimal of handling.

Here is a list of other uses of the blackberries fresh from the patch. Raw berries with or without sugar. There was berry cobbler, pies, jelly; jam, dumplings, sweet thickened berry pudding . Blackberry ice pops (after we got electricity and a refrigerator). One of my most favorite things was blackberry corn bread. My Grandma loved this cornbread and made it for us. The rest of the family did not like it, or at least not as well as Grandma and I did. I continue to make blackberry corn bread each year. I still love it and always think of my Grandma when I make it.

My Mama always insisted we "put up" one hundred quart jars of canned blackberries. If there was too much rain or not enough rain we may not be able to get that many berries. When there was a shortage we would have to try to fill the remainder of jars with other berries or fruits. Huckle berries were sought after and added to the blackberries when available. Dewberries, buck berries or even goose berries even though they were not the same color as blackberries.

There are two drawbacks to picking blackberries. First of all wild blackberries grow on plants that are covered with briars. The second thing is that the plants are covered with tiny red bugs called Chiggers here in the Mountains. In other places farther south they are just called Red bugs. If you have ever been bitten by a Chigger you know how uncomfortable you can be. The bugs are so small that you can't even see them with the natural eye unless you have very good eyesight. The bugs usually get under the arms, in the bend of the knee, under side. They also will "dig in" in the groin area and where clothes fit tight such as waistbands or sock tops. We used several different tactics to ward off the dreaded Chiggers. We would wear long sleeved shirts and long pants, yes even in July. Grandma would dip a rag into kerosene oil and rub the oil on the bottom of our pant or britches as was called then, and on the cuffs of our shirts. Grandma would sometimes even tie the rags dipped in the kerosene oil around our ankles and waist. The smell was so bad we didn't like to get close to each other.

Grandma always went with us to pick the berries; she would have a big ten-quart water bucket in one hand and a sharp hoe in the other hand. We kids carried several extra buckets, pails and pots. We stayed in the patch until our vessels were full or there were no more berries. The hoe was to make a trail through the tall weeds and briars; the best biggest berries always grew in the worst of places. The hoe was also an advantage over any snakes. There were plenty of Copperheads on our place. My Grandma could fatally wound a snake with one swift swing of the hoe. We would go on picking berries being more on the look out for the friends and family of the one who received the fatal blow.

How we kids managed to grow up with out being bitten is a miracle, often our dogs or animals were bitten.

We were told not to eat any berries until our buckets were full but we could not allow the biggest juiciest berries to go into the buckets. Our berry streaked mouth usually gave our secret away.

When we returned to the house with the berries, Mama was ready to "put them up". The jars were washed and scalded, or we continued with that task also. Mama did what is called the cold pack method of canning the berries. The berries were washed in cold water and placed into the clean jars to within one inch of the top. Cold water was poured over the berries. By placing a straight knife down the inside of the jar got out the air bubbles. A two-piece cap was used. The jars were placed into a canner with cold water coming to the shoulders of the jars. Allow the water to boil for 20 minutes with lid on canner. My Aunt Edna used hot pack method. You wash the berries in cold water. Measure the berries into a big kettle add ½ cup sugar to each quart of berries and cook until sugar is dissolved and berries are hot through. Ladle into the clean, scalded, hot jars and process in the hot water bath for fifteen minutes.

Jam was made by measuring the berries, placing in a large pot. The same amount of sugar was used as berries. This mixture was slowly cooked over low heat until thick. This could take hours. To speed up the process, the berry/sugar mixture with a small amount of water and a tablespoon or two of lemon juice added was boiled on med high heat with a rolling boil for about thirty minutes. Test jam by dropping a very small amount into a glass of cold water. If the jam stayed together and was firm it was "done". If the jam spread over the bottom of the glass, more cooking was needed. Whole berries were used to make the jam.

To make jelly the berries were boiled with a cup of water per gallon berries, until the berries were tender. The juice was removed by placing clean flour sackcloth over another container, and the berries and juice poured over the sack. The juice went through and the berries remained. If you wanted "clear jelly" meaning jelly with out pulp the bag was not squeezed. If you didn't have any lemon juice a little vinegar could be added or a handful of red berries could be cooked with the ripe ones. The red berries gave extra pectin, helping the jelly to jell. Jelly was made by the quick boiling method and tested same as the jam. The cloth with the berries could be squeezed allowing the pulp to be mixed with the juice to make a different texture of jelly. My Mama preferred the "clear jelly". My Aunt Edna preferred the jam and thicker jelly.

Blackberry juice for stomach ailments can be made the same as for the jelly, add a little sugar. It is easier on the stomach without much sugar. To drink the juice as a drink add more sugar as desired. To make ice pops, make as to drink and pour into ice trays. Place a pop sickle stick into each section, or use a plastic spoon. We used to save the pop sickle sticks at school from other people; we seldom had any money to buy ice cream. We took the sticks home and washed them to use in our pops.

To make blackberry corn bread, use firm berries mix a half cup of sugar and a half cup of flour toss the berries until well coated, Mix 2 cups cornmeal self-rising mix with half cup of sugar, 1 egg, and enough milk to make a batter. Bake in a cast iron pan until brown. Serve with butter and milk.

Blackberry juice makes a beautiful color for dyeing cloth. Make as for drinking juice. Do not dilute if a dark reddish purple color is wanted. Dilute for lighter color. Place the blackberry juice in a large pot. Add ½ to 1 cup of salt depending on amount of juice. Heat to boiling; add cloth in a steady even manner. Remove from heat before adding cloth. Leave until desired color or until cool enough to handle. Hang cloth to dry, being sure not to allow cloth to over lap. It is better to hang out side to drip dry. When dry rinse in cold water that has one half to one cup white vinegar added. Hang to drip dry again.

Blackberry dumplings; Place one quart of berries into a 6 or 8-quart kettle. Add 1 cup of water with 2 tablespoons corn starch mixed in. pour one cup of sugar over berries and cook until full rolling boil. Drop dumplings by the spoonful into the rolling boil. Cover the pot and reduce heat. Cook for fifteen minutes without lifting the lid. (To make dumplings mix one cup of self-rising flour with one half stick of butter or margarine. Mix well. Pour in enough milk to make a stiff batter) We just used fresh cream to make the dough, the butter and milk works very well.

Blackberry Thickening or Pudding

One quart can of blackberries; one cup of sugar one half-cup flour. Mix the flour into the juice of the berries. Pour all into a saucepan and cook slowly until thick. If too thick add a little water or milk. Serve over hot biscuits and butter. This was served at breakfast at our house. My brother Marvin loved it.

Blackberry –in- the- pan cake; Place one stick of butter in a baking pan and melt. Pour one cup of self-rising flour into a bowl, Stir in one cup of sugar and one cup of milk Add one beaten egg, mix well. Pour berries into pan evenly. Pour batter over berries slowly.

Bake slowly until golden brown.

Blackberry cobbler; one quart of berries one cup of sugar. A little water and a little corn starch. Pour into a baking dish. Make a pie crust type pastry. Cut into strips and cover top of berries. Bake until golden brown. To make a two crust pie; coat three cups blackberries with one half cup of cornstarch. Mix with one cup of sugar. Pour into an unbaked pie shell, cover with another crust. Slit the top in several places. Bake slowly until golden brown. Butter the top with butter when the pie comes from the oven by running a stick of butter over hot crust. Cool before serving or serve hot with vanilla ice cream.

We always managed to get a few chiggers. Those little red bugs would dig into the skin and try to hide. They were itchy. As we scratched the itchy we would scratch the chigger out. The itching continued for several days. You can rub calamine lotion or other topical creams onto the itchy spots. Nothing really helps much. Finger nail polish works best.

But I didn't have any nail polish until I was in the eighth grade. We were glad when blackberry-picking time was over. We enjoyed the berries year round.

A simple recipe that I use today for blackberry dumplings is; Wash four cups of fresh picked berries. Place berries in a pot, add one forth cup of water. Measure one and one half cups of powdered sugar (powdered sugar contains corn starch). Pour over berries, cover pot and cook until a good rolling boil. In the meantime, mix one package of White Lily Blackberry Muffin mix with one half cup of water. Drop by a small spoonful of mix into the berries, until all mix is used. Place lid on pot and simmer for ten to fifteen minutes. Lift pot lid and stir.

Serve hot or cold.

DOLLARS ON LITTLE LEGS

We just never seemed to have enough money for the necessities much less any money for extras. We were creative in the ways as to make a few dollars.

We helped our neighbor pick strawberries. Thelma Ammons grew tame strawberries for sale. She would pay us a quarter for each gallon of berries that we picked from her patch. The berries had to be clean and ripe, no bad ones. We were expected to do a good job. We picked and sold blackberries for fifty cents a gallon. We had to pick all that was needed by our family first.

Spring lizards would bring fifty cents a dozen for the big ones and seventy five for the jumbos. Fishermen liked to use the lizards for fish bait. We turned over every rock in the little branch that ran off from the spring, called the spring branch. Those little legs would move on. Daddy made a screen wire funnel to help with our production.

I usually carried the bucket and kept the lizards from crawling over the side and getting away.

My brothers did most of the catching. I do admit that at times I would have to help be a catcher. The money was divided in equal parts for each person involved. . People came from all over to fish in the Fontana Lake and bought the lizards for fish bait. We would hunt the same creek about twice a year. We were excited when an opportunity came to go in a creek that we had not hunted before. I was pretty scared to lift the rocks. I have an enormous fear of snakes, even small water snakes.

We had a big old tub that we could store the lizards in until we were able to take them to the boat dock or another place that sold fish bait. We put some moss and rocks in the tub and added some small red worms for them to eat. We could keep them for a long time as long as we kept the tub in the shade and left the screen wire cover on. In the edge of the spring branch was a good spot. Sometimes my Daddy went with us; He was really good at catching the slippery little crawlers.

If the light bill came and we had no money we would catch lizards to pay the bill. We had a lot of competition. There were several people doing the same thing we were doing. We were all just trying to get by. Sometimes we actually got to go fishing with the lizards as bait.

If I walk through a small stream today I will usually pick up a rock or kick one over just to see if there are any sizable spring lizards in the creek.

MEASLES

The summer of 1957 an epidemic of measles broke out in the community. Measles were more common back then than chicken pox are today. Emma, Marvin, Charles and I had all been exposed to the measles. My little sister, Dianne had been in the hospital at Asheville for two weeks with double pneumonia (both lungs were affected). Today that is known as bilateral pneumonia. Ann was very, very sick with a temperature of 105. She was packed in ice. The doctors did not give much hope for her recovery.

Mama stayed at the hospital all she could. Getting a way to Asheville back then was very hard to do. There just weren't that many people going to Asheville. When Mama got a way there, she stayed until someone came back for her. With neither of my parents having a driver's license or vehicle, it was rough.

My Mama was a woman with a lot of faith in God. She taught us kids to have faith also. Mama spent a lot of time on her knees

114

praying. Mama and Daddy both were going to the hospital together. Mama got up singing. She said that she knew in her heart that Ann was getting better. The doctors had kept Ann in a semi coma with medications. She had not spoken for days. Daddy asked her why she was so happy that day. She said she just "knew" that Ann had made a change for the better.

Sure enough when Mama and Daddy walked into her room, Ann cried out "Mommy".

She had improved. In a few days Mama brought her home from the hospital. She had only been home a couple of weeks when we were exposed to the measles. Mama did not want Ann or Linda to get the measles.

It was decided that since Emma was expected to take the measles at the same time the rest of us were, that my Grandma would take us bigger kids and go to Aunt Edna's and Grandma would help Aunt Edna look after all the invalids.

All went according to plan, all except for one thing. I did not get the measles. All three of the other kids took the measles. Every day I was checked thoroughly for the little red bumps. The other kids were in bed sick. Grandma was the nurse and doctor. I was up and going about as usual. I had to help Aunt Edna with the chores. We went to the barn one morning to feed the cattle and do the milking. I did what she told me to do, then as she was milking, I was suppose to hold the door of the stall shut so the cow could not get out if the mood struck her to try. I got tired of holding the door shut so I latched the door from the outside where I was stationed. I decided to go on to the house, never giving a thought as to how my Aunt Edna was going to get out of the barn.

Grandma asked where Aunt Edna was; I said, "She is still milking". An hour went by, Grandma was about to send me back to the barn to look for Aunt Edna. I started to go and saw her coming around the road. All of a sudden I realized I was probably in trouble for latching the gate and leaving the barn. My Aunt Edna was the type of person who attended to matters as they arose. Not one time did I ever hear her say "I'm going to tell your Mama on you"? I knew this would be no different. I was in for a spanking.

I decided to add fuel to the fire so to speak. I decided to go and hide. I went to the chicken house and opened the door to the feed room. I shut the door behind me and sat very still. After a while I heard my Aunt calling my name. I did not answer. Pretty soon my Grandma came looking for me, I still did not answer. After what seemed like a couple of hours gone by, my Aunt came back to the chicken house and called my name. I did not answer again. Aunt Edna finally said, "Bonnie Lou if you will come out I will not spank you." Oh boy! I decided now was the time to make an appearance.

True to her word, my Aunt did not say one word to me. My Grandma said" I think you had better carry in the stove wood. I did just that and every thing else that I could think of to do. I was very careful to make sure the chores were done just right. The measles lasted from ten to fourteen days. The invalids were on the mend. I was afraid I might get the measles all alone and have to stay in bed while every one else was up playing. That did not happen. I never got the measles at all. My Mama said that when I was a baby that I got real sick and broke out in a red rash. They thought that I had scarlet fever. Now they decided that I had the measles at that time.

All the precautions taken to keep my sisters free of measles were in vain. A few days later they were exposed to the measles by a child that came into the house with them. Ann and Linda both had a mild case of the measles. I still did not take them and to this day I have never had the measles.

APPLE TIME

We did not have a good apple tree on our new property. There was some land across the road from our place that was unattended. The owners lived out of state and never came around except once a year. There was a big apple tree a little ways up from the road.

My Grandma got permission from the owners to pick blackberries and harvest the apples from the big tree. The apples turned yellow in mid-summer. We kids took our one gallon metal berry bucket to the apple tree. We were told to gather the apples that had fallen on the ground. We quickly had the chore completed. The big old apple tree seemed to just spread her branches out as open arms for climbing. The tree forked fairly close to the ground. Climbing was not a problem. We actually ended up with some apples that just happened to get into our buckets by climbing the tree. I guess we must have accidentally knocked the apples from the tree.

If we were gone longer than what Mama or Grandma thought we should be, one of them would start hollering for us to come back with the apples. If no one hollered we would stay and play in the apple tree.

As soon as we returned to the house the apples were washed with cold water and the peeling began. The very best peels were saved to make jelly by boiling the peels with a quart of water. The peels were covered and left to steep until the apples were fixed. The peels were removed and jelly was made by using a little less sugar than juice. Boil for thirty minutes.

"An apple a day will keep the doctor away" may have been truer than we knew.

The apple has many uses. Eating raw was a good way to consume the apples. When cooked without the peeling, applesauce can be made. Boil the apples with a cup of water until apple slices are tender. Mash with a potato masher or run through a sieve. Do not add sugar until the applesauce is finished. Sugar added before boiling will sometimes cause the apples to hold their shape instead of cooking up fine. Cinnamon or all spice was added to enhance the flavor. This applesauce could be canned also. I like to add a teaspoon of vanilla to a quart of applesauce.

Fried apples were eaten for breakfast with hot biscuits and butter. Leave the peel on and slice and remove the core. Place a stick of butter or margarine in a cast iron fry pan. Place four cups of the sliced apples on the butter. Add one half to one cup of sugar and sprinkle cinnamon over the top. Place a lid on the pan and slow cook being sure not to burn. Do not stir, turn apples with turner. Remove lid and cook until sugar is caramelized.

Apples were peeled, sliced and dried in the sun to make dried apple pies and stack cakes. Place the slices on a cardboard with a cotton cloth over board, and place in the direct sun on a hot day. Bring indoors at night and repeat the next day. Continue for three or four days until apples are dry and leathery. Store apples in an airtight container such as a glass jar with a tight fitting lid. Now days they are stored in the freezer in plastic bags.

Every day we made a trip to the apple tree to retrieve any fallen fruit before the animals ate them. (Back then applesauce was referred to as fruit). To make apple butter cook apples tender as for applesauce. Put sugar and spices as desired and continue to cook until the applesauce has become very thick. Eat on bread or use to frost a cake. Vanilla flavoring can be added if desired.

A favorite question of us kids was "would you rather find a whole worn in the apple or a half of one?" I rather find a whole one, if I found a half of one I would know the other half had been eaten.

After a heavy rainstorm or winds we would again go to the apple tree to pick the apples.

To bake apples cut the core out with a sharp knife and place apple in a baking pan. Put butter and sugar, brown sugar or honey in the hole where the core was. Bake in a moderate oven until brown and bubbly. To make apple dumplings, grease the pan with butter, place apples in the pan. Fill the hole with a thin batter of flour butter sugar and milk, allowing the batter to run over the top of the apple and down the sides. Sprinkle more sugar and cinnamon over the batter and bake slowly for a long time.

Bleach Fruit is apple slices cured in a sulfur smoke bath. The apple slices stay nice and light colored. Peel and slice apples. In a five-gallon crock (we used) you can use smaller crocks, place a layer of apples in the bottom, leaving the middle open. Place hot coals in a tin can. Place tin can into another bigger tin can that has a layer of sand in the bottom. (You can also use an over sized coffee mug or teacup) . Use pliers for handling and cover face with a handkerchief. Place a clean flat rock in the middle of crock and put the tin cans on the rock. No rock needed if cup is used. Place some sulfur powder over the hot coals with face turned to the side. Quickly cover crock with a heavy towel. Allow twenty minutes for smoke to stop. Remove the can and repeat the process until all apples are used. If you do not have access to wood burned into hot coals, you can put fire to the sulfur. Be extremely careful. Remove the smoke cans and cover the crock with a piece of cotton fabric. Another method is to layer the apples in the crock. Place one cup of sulfur on the hot coals and leave for four or five hours. Be sure the sulfur is not too close as to burn the cloth on top.) Remove the tin cans and cover as before. Use the fruit directly from crock as desired. The weather today is not as cool as yesteryear. I recommend storing the fruit in the freezer. This fruit is supposed to keep colds and flue down if eaten every day. There is no guarantee but my Mother swears by it.

Apple pie: Make a crust using plain flour, Crisco or lard, mix well add enough cold water to hold together. Roll flat with a rolling pin or drinking glass that is smooth. Cut to fit pie plate with edges hanging over. Place in plate add four cups of apples that have been tossed with one half cup of sugar and two tablespoons flour. Place slices of butter at intervals over the apples. Sprinkle one-half cup of sugar that has cinnamon added over apples. Re roll the crust and place on top of pie. Crimp edges or press a fork around the edges to seal crust. Cut slits in top. Bake in moderate oven until golden brown (45-60 min.)

Apple crumb pie; Do it as for pie except no top crust. Mix together 1/2 cup butter one half cup flour one half cup oatmeal and one half cup of sugar. Spoon mixture over apples and bake.

Applesauce cake; bake a one box cake vanilla or yellow cake mix as directed on box in a flat baking pan. When tested done remove from oven. Spoon sweetened and spiced applesauce with vanilla added onto warm cake. Allow to completely cool before serving.

Mom's raw apple cake. This has always been a favorite at our house. Cream one and one half cups cooking oil with one and one half cups sugar and three eggs. Mix in three cups of self-rising flour and one tsp cinnamon. Add one tsp vanilla and stir well. Mix in three cups peeled chopped apples and one cup of pecans or walnuts. Pour into a greased baking pan and bake in a moderate hot oven for one hour or until done.

Icing. Boil one-half cup of water and two cups powdered sugar for five minutes. Pour over hot cake. Serve hot or cold.

Hot apple pie or cake served without ice cream is like a hug and no kiss.

Old time stack cake; 2& 2/3 cup of plain flour, one tsp of baking powder, one tsp each of ginger and salt, 1/2 cup of molasses, one cup brown sugar, ½ cup butter and 2 eggs. Cream sugar, eggs, butter and molasses together. Chill for 30 min. Divide into six parts, roll into balls. Press each ball into a greased pie pan until bottom is covered. (I prefer to roll out between two pieces of wax paper with a rolling pin and cut to fit pan.) Bake for fifteen minutes in a moderate oven 350_, place cake layer on a plate, spread on prepared applesauce. Stack and repeat until all layers are covered with applesauce on top.

One pound of dried apples cooked with a little water with a cup of sugar and a cup of brown sugar and one teaspoon of cinnamon. This is the old fashion method. I prefer to use fresh applesauce, about two quarts cooked with the sugars and spice until fairly thick.

Old time fried apple tarts (this recipe comes from Faye Cochran)

One quart of dried apples cooked into applesauce with sugar added to taste, and a little cinnamon. Make dough of plain flour with a little salt added Crisco and enough cold water to wet flour. Chill. Roll into 6-inch rounds but thin. Fill half with applesauce and fold other half over. Prick with a fork or squeeze together with fingers. Bake until brown in moderate hot oven; freezes well when there is any left over. Faye always makes these for homecomings and family get to gathers.

My mother fries her pies in butter; brown on one side and turn to brown the other side. She uses fresh or canned applesauce.

The apple has healing effects even when rotting. Place a little of the inside of a rotten apple on a boil or any skin condition for a drawing effect. It may also be used on other skin conditions such as cellulitis or infections.

GUINEA CHICKENS

My Grandma loved chickens of all types; she even loved sewing stuffed chickens. Her favorite real chickens were Guinea chickens. They were gray and white and squawked all the time. They were bigger than a regular chicken. The eggs were different; you could tell them from the other eggs. You could tell whether an egg came from which chicken. "Banties ", their eggs were small, Dominick were larger. The genuine laid a bigger egg. The duck egg was bigger than all the others. There were different colors of eggs. There were snow white, beige, dark brown and green eggs.

Grandma would get some corn in a bucket and go outside. She would rattle the corn kernels against the side of the bucket by shaking the corn around and around. Here those Guineas would come running and squawking. If you have never heard a Guanine squawk, you have missed something. Be glad. If you have not heard a whole flock squawk, you have really missed something. Be "gladder" that is the worst noise in the world, unless of course if you love chickens. My Daddy and Mama hated hearing the Guineas squawk. My Grandma was determined to have her Guineas, She loved the sounds that they made. Sometimes Grandma had only a few and other times she might have two dozen of the squawking birds.

The Guineas were a protective farm bird. No one could sneak up past those chickens. They were better than the farm dog to alert of any person or animal coming close to the house.

Grandma continued to keep her favorite chickens. The guineas would "take to the nest". They usually would not lay in the nests prepared for them. They chose to lay in the brush piles or under some tall weeds that had fallen over. We tried to find the nests with no luck most of the time. A hen would set on the nest for twenty-one days and babies would hatch out of the eggs that she was sitting on. "She was called an old setting hen".

A baby chicken pecks his way out of the shell. It was not good to try to help them crack the shell. They could die. We could not interfere with the birthing process. Most chickens are yellow at birth, but sometimes there would be a variety of colors. Black, yellow, brown or white, and even spotted ones. A baby chicken was called a bitty or chicks. A male chicken is a rooster. A female chicken is a pullet. A mama chicken is a Hen.

Other farm animals :

Cow = baby calf, a girl calf is referred to as a Heifer. That was also the name for a young female cow, which had not had a calf. After a calf was born she was just a regular cow. A boy calf was a bull. A year old calf is a yearling. A daddy cow was a bull. A steer was "fixed", meaning castrated. A mean bull was referred to as a brute.

Horse = baby, foal, colt girl is a mire or filly male is a stud a fixed male is a gelding

Hog = baby is piglet, a bigger baby is a sholt, mama is a sow, daddy is a boar

Goat = baby is a kid, mama is Nanny, daddy is a Billy

Sheep = baby is a lamb. mama is Ewe, daddy is a ram

Dog = baby is a puppy, mama is a bitch

Cat = baby is a kitten, mama is a pussycat, daddy is a tom cat

We have raised animals on a bottle from time to time. A calf needs a big nipple, and one to two quarts of milk at a time. A pig needs a smaller nipple and will take about eight ounces at the beginning. Puppies drink about two to four ounces at beginning. Kittens drink a small amount. It was always fun to feed baby animals. After awhile it got old. We were glad when the animal could be weined and eat normal food.

FISHING ON FONTANA LAKE

This was going to be our first time going fishing on the Fontana Lake. My Daddy's family had been relocated to the Need More Community from Bluff Branch down at Bushnell, N. C. after being forced to sell their land to make way for the lake. My Daddy and his family loved their old home place and hated to give it up. They missed their other family members who relocated to other areas.

That is just the way things were. All might as well make do with what is available. The Fontana Lake is now available for fishing. My Aunt Nancy Jane King had invited our family to come to her house for an all night fishing trip for the men. Mama, Grandma and us kids were to stay all night with Aunt Nancy at the house.

Aunt Nancy was married to Uncle Rufus King (we called him Uncle Ruff). They had four children, Ollie who was married and lived elsewhere, Floyd who was married to Virginia Breedlove of the Maple Springs Community. They lived on the road to the left of the

Maple Springs Baptist Church. Their children were R.V. and James (later Brenda came along). Marie was away at college. Clifford was at home; he was a year older than my brother Marvin.

Floyd came to our house and took our family to Aunt Nancy's. We seldom got to go there for a visit. They lived in the Lauada Community on a dirt road off to the left on the same road as the Sawmill Hill Church. There was a way to reach their house by walking but it was a long ways to walk. We could walk down the river to the Sawmill Creek swinging bridge and walked across the bridge and down the river on the other side and up to the house.

Aunt Nancy was my Grandma's oldest daughter, and Grandma did not see her very often.

We all happily piled onto the back of the truck, clad with pillows, blankets and fish bait that we kids collected.

There were red worms or night crawlers, minnow s that had been seined out of the creek that went by our house, and bee nests that we had recovered from the bees. That was tricky work at times. A long stick was used to loosen the wasp nest and make it fall to the ground. We snatched the nest and ran with it. Holding a cup of gasoline under the entry to their nest after dark could get a hornet's nest. Bees go to bed early. The fumes made the bees come from their nest and fall into the gasoline and die or they would just die from the fumes and fall out. Their nests were built above ground usually on a tree branch. Yellow Jackets usually built in low underbrush or in the ground. Gasoline was poured on the ground and set to fire. When all the bees were out, the nest was dug from the ground. The unhatched larva was used as bait to fish. Caution had to be used, as bees would continue to hatch out of the nest after it was collected.

When arriving to Aunt Nancy's house the whole bunch of us walked down a road about three quarters of a mile to the lake. We each had a cane pole with a string tied onto the small end and a fishhook was attached to the string. Bait of some kind would be put on the hook. The hook was then dropped into the water. We kids fished this way on the bank, while Uncle Ruff and my Daddy fished from his home made wooden boat.

Uncle Ruff had spent many hours working on his boat. Two large boards were used for the sides; the front went together in a V. There was a backboard about four feet wide. The boat was bottomed with wide boards and the cracks were filled with tar or some pine pitch. The boat was tapered from front to back. There were seats made by placing a board flat down on top of the sideboards. One at the back, one in the middle and one near the front of the boat. The cracks were filled with tar or pitch to keep water out and keep the boat afloat. Some water would seep into the bottom and it would be dipped out with a bucket carried in the boat. Oars or paddles were hand made from a thick board and carved down with a knife and smoothed with a piece of glass.

We kids were fishing; we had to be careful not to "catch each other". We caught several nice brim. My Uncle Ruff (who by the way was considered the best fisherman in theses parts of the country, well at least the best fisherman known by our family), and my Daddy brought the boat back to the bank and tied it to the tree where the boat was tied before. The place the boat was tied depended upon the rise and fall of the lake. The Fontana Lake does not stay full the year round. The lake rises in early spring and goes down in the fall. The men had caught a good string of fish. We all walked back to the house.

The men cleaned the fish, meaning they skinned the fish, took the insides out and cut the fish into small pieces to be fried. The water system was very neat. They had a hand pump that pumped water from the ground. With each up and down motion of the pump, a stream of water would make a gurgling sound, and then a swishing sound and water would jump from the spigot end of the pump. I thought that was a wonderful way to get water, I carried water in a ten quart water bucket from the spring to the house. I volunteered to get the water, I loved using the pump. The men washed the fish in cold water and filled a bowl with cold water to soak the fish in until frying time.

The women were getting supper ready. My Aunt Nancy was well experienced in frying fish. She took the fish from the water and put them in a mixture of whipped eggs and milk. Then the fish pieces were dredged in a cornmeal and flour mixture. Hot grease was waiting in a cast iron frying pan on the wood-burning cook stove. Potatoes were simmering on the back of the stove. Cole slaw was being made from a cabbage gotten from the vegetable garden. Green beans were ready to go on the table. Corn bread was nearly ready. I set the table in the dining room. We did not have a dining room. We ate in the kitchen at our house.

Aunt Nancy dropped a piece of coated fish into the hot grease and a sizzling sound came from the frying pan. The same sound came with the addition of each piece of fish. Salt and pepper were added to the fish. Shortly an aroma of the best kind arose from the frying fish. My Grandma mashed the potatoes, took the corn bread from the oven and sat the food on the table. Mama was helping get drinks poured and corralling all us kids to the wash basin to" wash up ". More water to be pumped, and of course every one wanted to pump the handle of the water pump.

Aunt Nancy had us all gather around the table and she sat a big platter of golden brown fried fish in the middle of the table. After grace was said we began to pile our plates as the food was passed around. (The prayer was referred to as grace). I couldn't wait to taste that fish. It was so wonderful. I ate a good mess of those fish. (A mess means I ate more than one helping, a mess was considered to be all one wanted of a particular food.) As a matter of fact I took the last piece of fish from the platter. I was later reprimanded by my mother. She said "you do not take the whole last piece of food from the platter, you cut it into two pieces and take half.) Well that was news to me, at our house we took the last piece if we wanted it, usually some one wanted it. That was a lesson in manners that has stuck with me ever since, well when eating at someone else's house any way.

Uncle Ruff and my Daddy were on the front porch talking about the fishing trip for the night. I decided I wanted to go with them. Daddy first said no, but uncle Ruff came to my rescue. "Yeah, you can go if you can stay awake all night and bait your own hook." I had never stayed awake all night before, but I thought that I could do it. Then Mama had to be told the good news. I am sure if I had asked my Mama first I would never have been allowed to go. I did not ask her, I just calmly said," Uncle Ruff said I could go fishing with him and Daddy tonight." My Mama wasn't used to family members going out on the lake in a flat-bottomed wooden boat, or any other way. She was very reluctant at first. After all the "you'll fall in, you can't stay awake all night, you will be in the way "stuff was said. Uncle Ruff said "she will be fine, I haven't lost a youngen yet". Mama finally gave in. I was going fishing on the lake in the boat for the night.

We got every thing ready, Mama gave the command to Daddy to watch me and not let me drown about fifty times before we started on our way. We untied the wooden boat that was still right where we left it earlier that day. We had a lantern, cobalt lamp that was a small metal device. The tank was flat bottomed about two inches tall with another two-inch tank that screwed into the bottom tank. About four-inch reflector plate was attached to the upper tank. A flint was used to make a spark. A tiny hole was in the center, which allowed the fuel to emerge as a flame when lit. Cobalt fuel was a very powerful chemical when mixed with a liquid, it became dangerous. A bluish color flame gave light as a little torch .My Daddy always stressed the danger of misuse. There was a little handle, which would be held by the hand, or hang from a nail, be worn on a hardhat or side of a board. The flat bottom allowed it to sit on a level surface. Another type of lantern was a kerosene lantern. This lantern was also metal. A little tank held the kerosene, a wire frame held the globe. A wick was lit inside the globe.

We fished first one side and then the other up near the head of the lake. Uncle Ruff knew right where to go to catch the crappies. We fished all night long. I stayed awake mainly because I was afraid to go to sleep. I did not have a life jacket on I loved to hear them talk of other fishing tales and tell stories of other things. The night passed rather quickly. We caught a bunch of fish. At daylight we tied the boat back to the tree and walked up to the house caring our stringers of fish. The men cleaned the fish as before. We ate breakfast and helped with the dishes.

We thanked Aunt Nancy and Uncle Ruff for inviting us for the trip. Floyd came and took us back home. That fishing trip was the beginning of many fishing trips for me on the Fontana Lake. None have compared to that first one. I have never been able to fry fish exactly like my Aunt Nancy's tasted that day.

"Give a man a fish and you have fed a man for a day.

Teach a man to fish and you will feed him for life."

Some folk believed if you ate fish, cabbage, corn bread, honey and sweet milk that you might die. I do not believe that to be true. My Grandma would not allow us kids to eat that combination of foods at one meal.

RAINED OUT CAMPING TRIP

My Daddy and brothers, Marvin and Charles were planning an overnight camping trip down on the Little Tennessee River. The walk was about two miles to where they wanted to camp.

I begged to go with the men folk. I was over ruled and this time I didn't have Uncle Ruff on my side. Daddy would not even relent. It was a boy's only camping trip. I was stuck at home.

The excitement ran high among the men folk of the house. All I heard was "camping trip, camping trip." Sibling jealousy, I was sick of hearing about the camping trip. The only good I could see would be a mess of fish for the whole family upon their return. I loved fried fish.

A trotline was going to be used to catch the fish. A trotline is a long piece of strong-corded carpenter twine. A loop was made in the line every three feet for the entire length of the trotline. A fishhook was tied onto an eighteen-inch piece of string and tied to the trotline through each loop to prevent the hooks from sliding together. Each hook was baited with your choice of bait. The same bait could be used on each hook or a variety could be used.

The trotline could be made to reach the entire width of the river, being tied to a tree limb at both sides of the river, and anchored with a heavy item or rock and one in the middle. A boat was needed to "put in" this type of line. Without a boat a shorter line could be put in the river by tying one end to a tree and tying a big rock on the other end and tossing the line out into the river, or by wading the rive and putting the line in the water. This was a little tricky, you had to wade the river above the hooks or run the risk of catching "the big one, your self" on the way back to the bank. It was a little harder to control the throw line, a strong arm had to be used. Practicing throwing big rock as far as you could helped to build up that kind of throwing ability. To determine if a fish was on the line, you could take hold of the line and if you felt a jerking or tugging on the line a fish had "taken the hook".

It is illegal to place a trot line across the entire body of water now, wheather it be lake or river.

The trotline was carefully packed in the tow sack (a burlap gunny sack used for carrying about everything). The fishhooks were gotten out and inspected. The hooks had to be sharp on the tip with the barb intact, and no rust. If the tip was not sharp enough, it would be sharpened by Daddy. A line of the same type as the trotline was used to tie the hooks onto the trotline. A swivel was the best choice to connect the fishhook line to the trotline. No swivels were available so the line with the fishhooks had to be tied onto the trotline. A double knot or slipknot could be used. A knot known as the blood knot made a very secure knot to hold the hook onto the line. Everything was placed into the tow sack

An old quilt and tarpaulin was folded and placed into another sack.

A blood knot was tied in this manner. The end of the eighteen-inch line was inserted through the eye of the fishhook and pulled out four inches (the thicker the line the more length needed). The four-inch line was then wrapped around the line beginning at the eye and going up for about six turns. The end was brought back down and inserted into the first loop above the eye, not the eye. The long end of the cord was pull taut (meaning leave no slack, secured firmly.) You need about one inch sticking out when finished. You might practice tying the knot ahead of time just to make sure.

My Daddy kept everything very neat. You could tie the line and hooks together now and stick the hooks in a piece of cardboard, or you could connect all after you got to the river.

A car-bide lantern was made ready and tucked away in safekeeping. That would be needed later as a light. An emergency flashlight was also tucked into the bag. Flash light batteries were very expensive and were only used in an emergency.

Mama baked a cake of corn bread and fixed up a half gallon of buttermilk to take along for supper. Coffee grounds and a tin one-gallon bucket would be used to make coffee over the open fire. A fry pan and a big slab of fat back along with salt, pepper and flour were all placed into a tow sack A dozen eggs were placed into three tin cups and put into the tin bucket.

Now for the bait it had been decided that chicken "inards" was to be used. Well chicken would serve two fold. Fried chicken for supper and bait for the trotline.

Charles was elected to get the bait ready. We helped him round up two chickens from the yard. If one chicken would "do" two would do better. With a piece of cord each chickens legs were tied together. The chicken could not get away.

Daddy and Marvin divided the load accordingly and place the tow sacks onto their backs. Charles had to carry the chickens. He could have put them into a tow sack as well, but Charles chooses to carry the chickens in his arms. One chicken under each arm. When Charles got tired of carrying them that way, He would hold them each in one hand. If He dropped the chickens they could not go any where with their legs tied together.

The journey of two miles thus began, as we waved to the men folk. I wasn't about to say, "have a good time", because I wanted to go along.

Excitement ran high as the men walked along and talked of their coming adventure of catching lots of fish.

The designated spot to fish was vacant. Depositing the camping "goods" on the ground one sack at a time ended with Charles placing the chickens on the ground "What is that smell, Charles do you know what those chickens did on you?" Charles did not care, he was camping and there was a river to clean up in.

They decided to put the trotline in first. The bait, wait, a chicken had to be killed and dressed. Daddy did the drudgery job while the boys looked on. The chicken was sliced and placed in the tin bucket with some salt and cold water (gotten from a spring close by). The "inards" were carefully hooked onto the fish hooks.

The trotline was placed into the water and secured to a tree and anchored down with rocks. With that job finished, "camp was made". Charles was sent to find dry wood for a fire; a pine chunk was needed for kindling. Marvin and Daddy hooked the tarpaulin. (Tarp). The corners were secured to a tree by tying a small rock in the corners. The corners were then tied to a tree limb. The front was tied up five feet off the ground. The back corners were tied close to the ground making a" lean to". A little ditch was dug in the ground directly below the tarp so just in case there was rain the water would run away from the sheltered spot.

Charles came back with wood several times. He had a good pile to make a nice fire. Daddy was a terrific cook in the kitchen as well as outside. He started helping his mother cook at a very young age. A fire was going soon. Daddy sliced part of the fat back and fried it "up real good and done" The grease was reheated while the chicken was dredged in the flour and seasoned with salt and pepper. The chicken sizzled as each piece was dropped into the hot frying pan. A few minutes later an aroma came out of the frying pan that could not be copied any where in the world except over an open fire in the woods. Mouths were watering. After several minutes of carefully attending the chicken each piece was turned to cook the other side to a golden brown same as before. Finally the chicken was done.

The grease was poured onto the firewood that would be used to start the fire up again in the morning. What a meal, open fire fried chicken with cornbread and buttermilk. Not a crumb of chicken was left. Half of the corn bread was saved for breakfast.

Not one little peep had been heard from the surviving chicken. I guess he was trying to be spared the fate of his brother. The chicken had wittnessed the demise of the other one. Only the male chickens (Roosters) were used for food. The female chicken called (Pullets or Hens) were used to produce eggs.

With tummies full and dark thirty settling in, it was time to stretch out the old quilt and get a few winks before the trotline needed to be "run" meaning checked for fish.

With all the excitement of the fishing trip keeping the boys awake the night before and the exhausting trip to the river and all the set up work, every one was tired and sleepy. Every one took their position on the quilt. Charles in the middle, his choice. All fell asleep in no time. The chicken did too. They continued sleeping until Daddy woke up when the rain was blowing in on his face. A rainstorm was in full force. Soon the water was overflowing the little ditch dug out with the sharp rock. Water was covering the camping spot like a slow moving shadow. In no time at all the quilt was soaking wet.

The boys sat up and saw water everywhere, they wondered if they were in the river. Daddy said "Boys lets get out of here and see if we can find a shelter. I ain't setting here in this rain." They gathered up the tow sacks, dripping with water and piled them up under the tarp. Charles had to collect that old wet chicken and tuck it under his arm again. The emergency flashlight had to be found. That kind of weather was no weather for car-bide lighting.

The men folk headed up the road about a forth of a mile and went into the woods where there was a rock cliff with an overhanging ledge. With water dripping from every one and, chicken included, the dry ground under the rock ledge was a welcomed site. Daddy shined the flashlight around to make sure no critters or snakes had the same idea as his. All was clear. There would be no more sleeping the rest of the night. They would just wait out the rain.

Each may have dozed off a little sitting in an upright position. Finally the morning light came and with the light the rain stopped. Daddy said, "Lets get going boys". Back down the road to the campsite they went. Yes, Charles still had that old chicken under his arm.

What a site awaited them. The quilt was completely covered in mud. The tarp had blown down all except one corner. Mud was over the rest of the tarp. The tarp had to be rescued; they were too costly to waste. The sacks were a mess. All food items were thrown out. That poor old chicken got to eat some watered down corn bread.

The trotline had been washed away with the currant. The quilt was deliberately forgotten lying under the mud.

With every thing thrown out except the fry pan and buttermilk jar; the tow sacks were still heavy. The tarp in one and everything else in the other. Yes Charles had to carry that old chicken the two miles back home.

We all went running to meet the fishermen knowing catfish bite better in muddy water. Much to our dismay there were no fish to eat from that fishing trip. I was surely glad I had not been given the privilege of going camping with the boys that time. They were a "sight for sore eyes". Mama made them breakfast while they demudded. It kind of served them right; I was in a dry bed all night.

I think that old chicken was the only happy camper in the group, he had made it back home safe and was carried the whole way. What a welcome sight the chicken coop was to him.

This story was told to me by Charles.

ROOT CELLAR PUNCH

My Daddy had a craving for alcohol that seemed to over take him and consume him from time to time. He struggled to let go of the cravings. Whisky making was a family trait passed from generation to generation. Some were able to over come the cravings, some were able to consume small quantities and others gave into more.

Daddy drank some whisky, but mostly he drank what was called home-brew or home brewed beer. Daddy used the five-gallon pickling crock to make his brew in. A glass a day was considered "good for you". The over indulging was what caused harm.

Sugar, malt syrup, yeast and water were the ingredients. All was placed into the crock, which was kept in the root cellar. A cotton white feed sack was placed over the top and tied with a string. A few days later the mixture would "work off"

My younger brother Charles and my sisters, Linda and Dianne decided to sample the home brew. They were outside playing below the house at the entry of the root cellar. Every little bit they would go into the cellar and get a dipper of the brew and drink it. Pretty soon the evidence started to show in their walk and talk. A lot of giggling was taking place and a stagger was in their walk. My Mama looked out the window and saw them playing and falling to the ground. She was not alarmed at first. The staggering became worse. Mama asked Grandma "do you think there is any thing wrong with the kids or are they just playing"? Grandma started to watch them. She said, "I bet they have been into the home brew". Mama went to investigate and sure enough they were under the influence of the root cellar punch. Mama made them go into the house and "sleep it off".

When my Daddy got home that evening, Mama was fit to be tied. She really gave Daddy a raking over. There was no more home brewed beer in the root cellar for a long time.

Daddy told me just a few years before he died that he guessed that was the maddest Mama had ever been with him.

MR. PEACH MAN

The most unusual thing about Mr. Peach Man was you never knew when he would bring a load of peaches by our home in the mountains of North Carolina back in the 50's. This particular year my Daddy was working around the house when Mr. Peach Man made his annual appearance. He could count on our family buying four or five bushel of his peaches. I heard my Daddy say "I will take ten bushel today." I saw this strange look come over my Moms face. I thought it was wonderful that we were getting so many peaches. My Mother always canned one hundred quart jars of peaches each year. She also canned one hundred quarts of several other items, some grown in the garden, others picked in the "wild" such as blackberries. Not knowing when Mr. Peach Man would arrive we were unprepared for so many peaches.

Right away we quickly consumed a few delicious ripe peaches. The peaches were free stones meaning the seed would be easy to remove.

The other group is known as clingstones or clings, meaning the fruit clings to the seed or stone and is very difficult to work with.

Then the work began. I had to carry water for all household needs. I filled up the big washtub, and added an abundance of soap powder. There were enough soap bubbles to do a week s wash. The Mason jar washing event was well under way. More water was needed to rinse the bubbles from the jars, still more water was needed to heat on the wood burning cook stove to scald the jars before placing the peaches inside the jar. Oh yeah, a big bucket of water was needed to wash the fuzz off every peach. Did I mention the water tank on the side of the stove had to be filled also?

The peach peeling was also off to a good start. My Mama, Grandma, and Daddy were sorting the peaches, peeling the ripest ones first. The jar washing was left to my brothers, Marvin and Charles and my sister Linda. I was the oldest girl at 12 years old; it was time for me to be taught the skillful art of canning, making jam and jelly. Today was my first lesson. I was given a not to sharp paring knife. My little sister Dianne, we called her Annie was nearly six years old. Every one had a chore to do, she was assigned the task of washing the peaches before they were peeled. This was an easy thing and a fun thing. My sister would pick up a peach and holding it about a foot above the water bucket would let go and the peach went splashing into the water. Water went everywhere. It felt good on my feet. The day was hot. The water was quickly disappearing which meant I would need to go back to the water supply for more water. My other job was to take the seed (or stone as my Grandma said) from the inside of the peach. Mama preferred or maybe I should say demanded the peaches be made into only two pieces. Two perfect halves (this was necessary to create a beautiful display in the jar). I cut around the peach following the seam, pulled the peach apart and popped out the single seed. With so many peelers, I had to work fast. I noticed the adults were taking the seed out of some of the peaches to help me keep up. My Daddy called the seed the pit. So now we have seed, stone or pit. You take your pick.

There was a certain container used in canning that held exactly seven quarts, the amount of quart jars one canner held at a time. When the container was full Mama took it into the kitchen. The peach peeling party took place on the front porch, which was why my little sister could get by with splashing the water everywhere. Today Mama asked me to come with her and help with the canning in the kitchen. We scalded the jars and she showed me how to place the peach halves into the jar. The cut side down, place four into the bottom of the jar. Stack each half on top of the one before and continue until the jar was full, all except one-inch headspace had to be left. If a peach half got turned over, cut side showing it had to be redone. Mama took great pride in the way the canned food appeared. As soon as seven jars were filled, hot syrup of water and sugar, which had been boiled, was poured over the peaches. The top was carefully wiped with clean damp flour sackcloth. The two-piece lid was securely attached. The jars were placed into the galvanized canner and water was added up to the shoulders of the jars. The peaches were cooked in a boiling water bath for 20 minutes. Mama took care of the canners and timed the process. By the time we got seven quarts ready the rest of the peeling party had another "run" peeled. My older brother had joined, taking over my place of removing the seed. This activity continued the rest of the day with only a short break for lunch. We were all so full of peaches we were not very hungry.

After the jars were boiled long enough, Mama removed then very carefully and placed the jars on to a table prepared with a heavy towel. As the jars cooled the lids went pop, pop, pop, Mama would know exactly how many jars had not sealed. By the end of the day we were all very tired. I forgot to tell you while I was carrying the water, my Grandma had picked out all the over ripe peaches and had placed them in a big pot with the exact amount of sugar to make peach butter. The pot had simmered all day with us stirring the peach mixture often with a large wooden spoon. This peach butter was now ready to place into a jar. The jar received the same treatment the other jars had received. These jars were inverted on the towel and left overnight to seal. The ones that did not seal were eaten for breakfast with hot biscuits.

The next day we started again with the same routine as the day before. When all the ripe peaches were worked up we would start on the green ones. The green peaches were peeled and left whole, no seed taken out. A mixture of cloves, cinnamon, vinegar and sugar was simmering on the stove. Yummy smell. The green peaches were placed into a large mouth jar and the spice mixture poured over the peaches, then processed as the others were. The only thing left were the peelings, which had been sorted as the nicest peelings were saved to make jelly. They were boiled "with a little water added" until cooked. The liquid was strained off and the peelings discarded. The same amount of sugar as juice was placed into a large pot and boiled for about 30 minutes. The thickened jelly was poured into prepared jars and processed same as the peach butter. The other peelings were taken to the pigs and chickens.

The next time Mr. Peach Man came to our house, Mama bought the usual four or five bushel. Never again did we get ten bushel of peaches at one time. We had more peaches canned than any other item that year.

I still like to make peach butter and jelly. I have to go to the Farmers Market to get the peaches. No Mr. Peach Man any more. I usually put the peaches for peach butter in the crock-pot to simmer for hours. The wonderful aroma takes me back to the front porch of our childhood home and the summer we canned peaches for two days.

PEACH TREE TEA

There are all sorts of teas on the market today. Blends and mixes not known to us back then. There was a "tea" then unknown to most today. We kids did not like that tea at all. It wasn't a drink, as we know tea. The peach tree grew long slim branches; one branch was all that was needed for this "tea".

The peach tree "tea" was a way of correction, a way of changing the attitude. changing the mind and maybe even changing ones life. We usually had to go to the peach tree and collect "our own hickory". I have had to go back a second time when I got a flimsy limb. We soon learned to get a "decent hickory" the first go around. In the story of my big brother is an example of Peach tree tea.

The peach tree limb was held in the dominant hand of the use or abuser depending on how you look at things. Mama and Grandma were both right handed. Their right hand gripped the thin hickory while their left hand held a firm grip on our left hand. They brought the hickory around and made contact with whatever part of our body that was vulnerable. We went round and round with the hickory making contact several times, leaving red streaks on our legs back and any where else not covered with clothing.

We would be screaming and hollering loud enough to alert the whole neighborhood, but no one seemed to hear or care. It was a normal every day routine at our house. I hold a high respect to the peach tree tea.

Social Services today would have a heyday if they were to witness such disciplinary efforts. I personally appreciate the discipline of my parents and grandparent, even if I do not approve of some of the methods used. There were other ways to be corrected, some even worse than the peach tree tea.

The peach tree does possess other benefits for human consumption and use. The peach tree leaves have been used to make a poultice to reduce fevers and help relieve congestion. For added results puree the fruit and drink slowly. The peach is a wonderful tasting fruit. The fruit is considered "easy on the stomach" thus being useful to settle a sick stomach almost as good as the blackberry juice.

The peach tree leaf poultice is made by crushing the leaves and soaking in vinegar and apply to chest and throat for congestion or applied to forehead for fever. Another way to make a poltice is boil the leaves and use the water to wet a compress and use on forehead.

Peaches are best when eaten in the raw stage, however they have a very good flavor canned. The peach can also be frozen either peeled and sliced or left whole. They take up a lot of room in the freezer when left whole. I still manage to save room for at least a dozen whole peaches each year in my freezer. When I am ready to eat the frozen whole peach I hold it under warm running water for a little while and remove the peel by hand. I eat while mostly frozen.

DEHART REUNION

My mother was Pauline Dehart before she married my Daddy. The Deharts have held a family reunion every year the second Sunday of August forever. Actually the first gathering was in May to celebrate Martha Dehart's birthday, which was May 18. It was decided to change the gathering to August because there were no vegetables to prepare. In August the garden would be "in". The gathering changed from a birthday party to a family reunion.

Martha Dehart was the wife of Martin Dehart. Their children were Charlie, Jake, Vance, Dave and Victoria. Charlie Dehart was my Mothers Father and my Grandfather. There were cousins by the dozens. Aunts, and uncles. There was Martin, John, Martha, Mary; the list goes on and on, Burin, Richmond, Perry. Lucy, Dexter, Jo, Mildred, Cleve, Kelse and Irene. I wish I could remember all of them. There was Liza, her brother and sister. There were a lot of people .

The Dehart reunion was the only family reunion we were invited to attend. We kids looked forward to it; there was so much good food. We always had food to eat but nothing like the bounty on the tables at the reunion. The best part for us kids was the drinks. There were gallons and gallons of lemon aide. There were bottle drinks in tubs of ice. We each could have a whole drink and not have to share. We could go back for seconds and thirds if of course Mama or Grandma didn't see us. Grandma was a little stricter than Mama. I remember drinking three drinks one day. I probably would have gone for more if Grandma had not stopped me.

There was plenty of pies and cakes, lemon, chocolate, apple. There was just so much good food a kid could just eat until you thought you were going to pop. Then there was singing kind of like a church service. Then the singing stopped and people talked and talked until away up in the evening. We would gather up the containers and go home promising to all be there again the next year.

The reunions were held at the Hightower Church when I was young. They changed from place to place and back to Hightower. Then for several years the reunion was held at the Cold Springs Church. It became difficult to not disturb the church service. We would have to wait until the service ended and then it would be later getting started.

From time to time there have been some problems with in the reunion. We have had people show up at the reunion and claim to be

Dehart descendents; no one knew where they came from. We have had one such person attempt to take over the reunion and eliminate people from their elected positions. He is no longer involved.

The reunion moved to Deep Creek Rec. Park pavilion and again back to Cold Springs.

Now back to the rec park.

Each year a prize was given to the youngest and oldest Dehart relative.

This past year 2004 the youngest relative was a set of twins, age 3. Descendants from the Charlie Dehart family. Aunt Edna being Charlie's daughter is their great grandma. Emma Sutton Waldroup their Grandma and Jeff and Lisa Waldroup, their parents. The twin's names are Jacob and Jesse Waldroup. The twins along with their big brother Matthew sang some beautiful songs for us and did a terrific job.

We were saddened by the death of Liza Seay who had kept the reunion alive and knew every single person and how they fit into the puzzle. She was the secretary for many many years. We miss her terribly. Liza straightened out all the kinks and, kept the records straight and straightened out any person with ideas of change. How will we ever manage without Liza? What a dear lady, I am proud to be a relative of such a lady.

Kim Lequire, Granddaughter of Charlie Dehart is the president now, Kim's sister Emma Waldroup serves as vice president. Emma did her time as president for several years. The secretary now is Kathy Slate

There were several faces there that I did not know. There were Dehart relatives there that did not attend years ago. Again there was lots of good food and drinks. Everyone had a good time. The reunion for next year was set for the same place same time. Emma Waldroup modeled the tee shirts that are about ten years old. New shirts are planned for next year. Mark your calendars for the second Sunday in August and plan to be a part of the Dehart reunion if you are a descendant of the Deharts. We would like for more people to attend.

THE VISIT

During the summer between fourth and fifth grade, my parents were going to visit my Aunt Merrill and Uncle Wayne Ammons who had moved to Conley's Creek up past Whittier. That seemed like a very long ways off to me. We kids always stayed at home with Grandma when our parents went somewhere.

I had never been to visit My Aunt and Uncle in Whittier. I begged Mama to let me go. I figured the other kids could keep Grandma company. I begged and begged. My heart was really set on going. Mama was the type of person who would say no a half dozen times and then say yes. I kept begging her.

Finally I started crying my heart out, I truly wanted to go more than any thing. Finally Mama agreed that I could go. I was so excited. I would have something to tell the class on the first day of school. The teacher always asked each student what he or she did over the summer, where they had gone. I had never been anywhere to tell about.

We finally got to the place we were going. It was a beautiful place with a rolling yard that had grass growing in the yard. We swept our yard. This one was mowed. I enjoyed seeing my cousins and especially Aunt Merrill. Aunt Merrill has always been a really sweet person. Very calm and easygoing, sort of the way my younger brother Charles has been.

The best part of the visit was when Aunt Merrill asked if I wanted to go out under the grape vine and pick some grapes. Did I ever? Grapes were one of my favorite things and we didn't have a real good vine at our house. Not then. I picked and ate all the grapes I could possible hold. They were so delicious. There was Concord purple grapes and pink grapes. I was in grape heaven. We picked some grapes to take back home to the rest of the family.

On the way back home I wasn't feeling too good. I always got carsick and I had eaten too many grapes. By the time I got home I did not want to see another grape that day.

Sure enough when my time came to tell where I had gone during the summer, I proudly said "I went to see my Aunt and Uncle." The teacher asked where they lived. I again proudly said Whittier N. C. You would have though that I had said something very funny. The kids started laughing and making fun of me. My teacher got every one quieted down. I was so embarrassed. I had never been on a vacation before. I did not know that people actually went on trips over the summer.

For a long time some of the kids would walk by me and say "Whittier" real low so the teacher did not hear and the ones sitting or standing close by heard. They would erupt into a full blown laughing cession. I was humiliated. Finally as the year wore on the harassment stopped. I did not have a story to tell the next year or the next or ever again. Kids can be so cruel.

I still think of that trip as a fun trip even if I did eat too many grapes. I still love grapes today.

SECTION SIX:
FALL

PINE KNOT KINDLING

Mama cooked all our meals and heated all the water for our family's use on the wood-burning cook stove in the kitchen. The house was heated with a big potbelly stove in the living room, which used wood or coal. This stove was referred to as the heater. The wood used for cooking was called stove wood; the wood used to heat with was called heater wood.

The firebox in the cook stove was small and the wood was cut into small, short sticks about two inches thick and twelve to fifteen inches long. The heating wood could be much larger. The heater would keep a fire all night long if the damper and vents were closed and the stove "filled up" with green wood at bedtime. The next morning you opened the damper and vents, put more wood in to the stove and soon the room was toasty warm. The cook stove would not keep a fire all night. Each morning my Daddy (later this became my brother Marvin's chore) would start a new fire in the cook stove. This meant good kindling must be kept. We kids had to get off to school each day, the school bus arrived at 7:10 each morning. This meant Mama had to fix breakfast at a certain time each day to feed us before we went to school. The best kindling was pine knots. The rosin in the pine caught fire very quickly. This wood is sometimes called "fat wood". We used a lot of dry wood in the cook stove to cook breakfast as dry wood heated faster than green wood.

We combed the mountainsides in search of the prized kindling. Dead pine trees were scarce back then. (Now the pine trees are down everywhere, not so back then). We carried a "tow sack" to collect the smaller chunks. The larger ones were tumbled down the mountain and dragged to the house. My Daddy chopped the chunks into small pieces. The kindling was used very sparingly. A tiny bit would start a fire. The Chestnut trees were dead and dry on the ground due to some disease to them. This made really good stove wood to go with the kindling. A few green sticks were added to the dry wood to keep the fire going. Stove wood was divided into three groups. Dry wood, seasoned wood and green wood. Dry wood made a quick hot fire. Dry wood was the trees that were "down, dead and dry" Seasoned wood did not burn as fast as dry wood but faster than the green . Seasoned wood was wood cut about a year ahead and left to dry some. Green wood was cut and used with the sap still in the wood. The sap would seep from the wood as it burned making green wood last longer while burning. If the stove was too hot a stick of green wood was added. For canning a hot fire was needed to get the canner boiling. To cook for a long amount of time the green wood would keep the pot boiling. The oven temperature was as important as the stove top. Water heated in the reservoir at the far side of the stove to wash the dishes.

We enjoyed going into the woods to help locate the good wood. We made a game of it, even though it was a very serious chore. We had no other way to heat our home or cook the meals. For a long time all the wood was sawed by hand, using a cross cut saw, (a saw blade about five and half feet long with a handle on each end.) Two people were needed to operate the saw. My brothers learned to use this saw early in their life. The power saw was a treasured possession after my Dad bought one. The new saw reduced the amount of time needed to "get wood" drastically, although the chore still remained a big job.

There was a wooden box beside the stove that held the wood. Each night the box was filled, this was a chore shared by my brothers. My chore was carrying the water and washing the dishes. I learned to cook at an early age. My Mother had a heart condition that made her sick a lot and she needed help. I am glad that I did learn to cook early. I still love to cook. I have no problem cooking for a large crowd. There was always at least eight and more at times, to cook for in my family back then.

Food cooked using a wood stove tastes better than food cooked on an electric stove. I have an old wood cook stove in my kitchen. In winter I love to start a fire (I still use the pine knots same as of old) in it and cook a meal. I have to be very careful or I burn the food. Once you get a good fire going, the food cooks much faster. The entire surface of the stove is a cook area, making a lot more space for the pots and pans. I enjoy canning meats in the winter using the stove. The first part of the stove is very hot. Toward the back and to the side makes a wonderful place to simmer foods. I am thankful for my electric range and bake ovens with the ability to maintain even heat. I am thankful for not having to get wood as we did back then. Yet when I make a fire in the wood cook stove I am immediately taken back to my childhood days of long ago. I can almost smell the pinto beans cooking.

DADDY KNOWS BEST

My little brother Charles was about six or seven years old when someone gave Daddy a tricycle to take home to Charles. All Charles ever had was what was left of the tricycle that me and Marvin had fought over many times. Charles was so proud of his "new old" trike.

Charles was inseparable from that trike. He was on it constantly riding everywhere he went. His legs were working really hard to give his butt a ride.

Daddy was going to go up in the woods to cut some firewood and the boys had to go with him. Charles got that trike headed toward the pasture, peddling away. Daddy said "son leave that thing here, you will get it torn up in the woods" Charles said no, I will be real careful I won't tear it up. Daddy said "you had better leave it like I said." Charles had a mind of his own; He had no intentions of leaving the tricycle to the hands of Linda and Ann.

Charles was peddling as fast as his legs could go. The pasture got steeper the farther you went. It was straight up farther on. Charles rode as far as he could and then he pushed the trike the rest of the way to the woods. Daddy was firm this time; he made Charles leave the trike at the edge of the woods.

The men folk worked a few hours rounding up and cutting some wood. On the way back Charles ran on ahead and jumped on the tricycle and headed it in the direction of home. He did not have to peddle. It was straight down hill. The trike rolled on its own. The farther, the faster. Charles was just "going with the wind".

Near the bottom of the pasture the front wheel went into a hole in the ground. The rest of the trike and Charles could not stop. Charles went hurling through the air at a great speed, head over heels and came to rest in a heap where a cow had recently left behind a fresh cow "pie" Charles got up off the ground, head spinning a little bit. Embarrassment soon settled in. Daddy and Marvin was a wittness to the whole thing.

The back wheels were standing in the air still turning. The seat was bent. The steering column had broken and the handlebars had taken a little trip of their own. Charles found them about ten feet away from the rest of the trike I mean what was left of the trike. Realization set in with Charles. He knew his trike had been demolished and no more riding for him. One good days worth of riding was all that trike would be good for. Here one day and gone the next.

Daddy said, "Son are you hurt"? Before Charles could even answer that question Daddy said,"son I told you to leave that thing at the house, you should have listened to me."

Charles was a little shaken up but most of his entire prized trike was gone. He really did wish he had listened to Daddy. After all Daddy does know best.

BARN EVENTS

My Aunt Edna and Uncle Lloyd raised cattle. There were always several farm animals, which needed shelter and food. The cattle were put into the stalls at night.

In the fall after the leaves had fallen from the trees, the leaves were raked into a big pile and carried to the barn. We filled up tow sacks (burlap) to carry the leaves to the barn. The barn sat upon a hill to the left of the state road, across from and above the house. The dirt road that wound around through their property was below the barn. (Emma and Leonard Waldroup had the hill dozed off and built their house close to where the old barn used to be.) A grove of pine trees grew between the road and the barn and on out into the pasture, the leaves from the pines (Pine needles) mixed with other leaves made a good bed for the cattle.

After school I rode the bus home with Emma to help with the leaf gathering. We had great fun raking the leaves. We would get a big pile and "take a run ago" and land in the leaves. That was short-lived because Aunt Edna wanted us to hurry. Dark would set in soon. We continued with pilling as many leaves into each sack as was possible and carried or dragged the sack to the barn. We emptied our sacks and repeated the process until enough leaves had been placed into the stall so as each animal had a nice bed to lie down in. This process was repeated about once a week because the cattle would stomp on the leaves and they would just sort of disappear.

My Aunt Edna sold cows milk to the Nantahala Diary, which used the milk to make butter, buttermilk, cream, ice cream and pasteurized milk. We thought the milk was already pasteurized because the milk cows were kept in the pasture. We were wrong about that.

The milk was collected from the cow by Aunt Edna. We were later taught the art of milking. Several buckets were taken to the barn. One bucket held warm water, which was used to wash the cow's utters .A white flour sack was then used to dry the utters. A ten quart water bucket was placed on the ground beside the cow to be milked. While the cow ate her food Aunt Edna milked her. Aunt Edna sat on a little stool. The bucket kind of sat between her feet. Aunt Edna took an utter in each hand and with a downward motion while squeezing the utter she would bring the milk into the bucket. This was done by even steady squeezes and strokes. Almost a steady stream of milk came pouring into the bucket. You see Aunt Edna was an experienced milker.

Two or three cats would be sitting close by awaiting for the right moment when milk would come their way. Aunt Edna would turn toward the cat and say "okay Tom get ready." That old Tomcat would open his mouth and Aunt Edna would send a stream of milk right into his mouth. Each cat was called by name and the scene repeated. This happened several times, until she said, "that's enough". If the milk splattered on the cat, he would lick himself trying to collect every drop.

When all the milk was extracted from the two utters, Aunt Edna would reach under and get the other two and repeat the process. Usually the cats were lingering with the anticipation of getting another gourmet treat. The stripping came last. Aunt Edna would squeeze each utter a little more to extract all the hinder milk known as the cream. Each cow was milked in the same manner. The cats stayed to the finish. The milk was carefully carried to the house in the buckets.

Once the milk was safely in the house it was strained. A thin white cloth was placed over a wide mouth glass jar and the milk poured into the cloth slowly. The milk flowed through the cloth any particles gotten into the bucket were caught in the cloth. Maybe nothing was collected or maybe a piece of leaf debris. The milk was placed into the spring box to cool. The milk buckets were washed and the cloth strained was washed and ready for the next milking. The cows were milked twice each day.

A truck came from Franklin, N.C. to the house and picked the milk up. The milk was poured into insulated tin containers called milk cans. Each container held ten gallons of milk. The truck came on Monday, Wednesday and Friday. There would usually be three containers ready, (thirty gallons of milk.) The diary truck started leaving the containers for Aunt Edna to have ready. It would take two men to load the containers. Milk sold for 35 to 40 cents a gallon. Jersey cows were good milk producers.

At one time Aunt Edna just sold the cream which brought a higher price but there was less volume.

Old Time Ice- cream

Freeze the heavy cream in metal ice trays until frozen solid. Remove from ice trays and place into a large bowl. Mix sugar, eggs and vanilla into the frozen cream with a hand mixer. Continue beating the mixture until frothy. This was a hard task because the hand mixer was what was called an eggbeater. We did not have an electric mixer or ice-cream maker. After the mixture was thick and frothy it was poured into a bowl and again placed in the freezer section of the refrigerator and frozen. A real treat. Strawberries or other fruit could be chopped and added just before the second freezing.

CORN FIELD FINALE

Several uses of the corn have already been mentioned. Just before frost was expected the stalks of corn were cut off a little above the ground with the ears still on the stalk. The stalks were bundled together and placed around a stick anchored in the ground. This was tied securely with a rope. Pumpkins were stored inside the corn shock to keep from freezing. Another way was to clip the tops off just above the ears of corn. The tops were bundled together and kept in the barn and feed to the cattle. The blades of corn left were pulled off the stalk and bundled into fodder and also used for feed.

There was a pest living on the corn blades called a packsaddle. There is no such word in the Webster Dictionary. The packsaddle resembles the woolly worn except it is a light color. Some have a darker spot on their back that resembles a saddle. Others are white or light yellow. The woolly worm is usually dark brown and black. Every person who has ever been bitten or stung by the packsaddle knows to keep an eye out for the critter. The sting of the packsaddle is very painful. We would usually manage to be in direct contact with at least one or two a year. Once we were stung we made a high dive toward the house to find Grandma. Grandma dipped snuff and she would put her finger into her mouth and pull out a pinch of wet snuff. One dab and the pain would begin to decrease. That old snuff was wonderful stuff.

After the fodder was all gathered and placed into bundles we would collect a bunch and carry to the storage place. After frost the corn was gathered. This was a family affair also. Most of the chores were family affairs.

The best ears of corn were saved to make corn meal at the gristmill. A portion of meal was given in exchange for grinding the corn. The kernels had to be shelled from the cob to make corn meal. Some good corn was saved to make hominy. The corn meal had many uses. Some of the best ears of corn were saved for seed for the next years planting.

The cornmeal was sifted through a wire sieve, the finer meal went through and the course part called bran stayed in the sieve. The bran was tossed out to the chickens.

Uses of the corn meal was cornbread, corn mush, corn fritters, coating for frying foods, for thickening soups, crusts for meat pies and berry cobbler. Hush puppies, fry bread, pancakes, pone bread, corn meal gravy and the list go on. Salt, soda and baking powder were added to all breads made from the corn meal. I have left those items out of the recipes listed because self rising corn meal on the market today have those already added into the cornmeal. Corn whiskey was another use of the cornmeal.

Some uses of the cobs have already been mentioned. The red corn cobs could be boiled and make a reddish jelly. Corncob dolls were popular and fun to make.

The shucks were feed to the cattle dry or green. The stalks had uses too. They could be ground into cattle feed along with the corn. Any stalks or shucks left in the field was plowed under and they supplied nutrients to the field. We kids made corn stalk swords. They were not too dangerous and were a lot of fun.

Corn Shuck Doll

To make a corn shuck doll using a whole ear of corn: Pull shuck back but leave connected to the ear of corn. Divide the corn into three parts. The head the smaller part next to the attached shuck. Remove one row of kernels all the way around the ear. Make a body the same way. The last part should be the biggest of all three. Bring the shuck around the head and tie with string. Make a wire for arms and cover with more shuck. Place arms above body and secure by wrapping the wire around the cob, continue with the body, tying the shuck in the space where the kernels were removed. Trim the bottom of the shuck evenly with scissors. Make clothes and hat of choice for doll to wear. Paint facial features with a pin.

Corn meal gravy: Place two tablespoons of bacon drippings in fry pan. Salt as desired. Add pepper with the milk. Add a handful of corn meal cook until brown. Add one to two cups of milk depending on how thick you want the gravy. Cook until done. This gravy is really good over fried potatoes.

For fried corn bread: Mix 2 cups of self-rising corn meal, one half cup of flour. Add boiling water to make thick mush-like dough. Beat the egg in a separate bowl. Stir egg into the hot mixture quickly. Drop a heaping tablespoon of batter onto a hot greased skillet. Add chopped onion to batter and fry in deep fat for hush puppies

For a heavier crust on corn bread generously grease the cast iron skillet, bake in a hot oven.

Cornmeal is still a staple food source today. There are so many things to be made from cornmeal. There are very few gristmills available today for public use. I know a few people who still grind their own corn.

INTRUDER

The house, barn, pigpen, garden and crops took up all of the level land on our property. My favorite spot was on a hill above the pigpen in the woods. There was a little open level spot up the hill a little ways. I loved to go there. I called this spot my "play house". The roof was a canopy of Mt. Laurels and Hemlock trees. The floor was a carpet of pine needles and other leaves. The walls were the dense forest growth.

I would take a book there to read and sometimes took my younger sisters to play. A big rock served as a balcony. We sat there with our legs hanging over the side. The place under the rock was checked each time before sitting on the rock. My friends liked to go there to play also.

One day there was an intruder invading my spot. A black fuzzy ball was away up in a tree very close to the spot. My Mama started hollering for my Daddy to bring a gun. Mama was hanging out clothes to dry on the clothesline. My Daddy finally came out of the house with a gun in his hand. He was putting a shell into the gun. My Mama was hollering and pointing in the direction of the big fuzzy ball. "It's a bear"! There had not been any bears spotted on our property before, so my Daddy probably did not expect to see a bear. Daddy only brought one shell from the house. My Daddy was "a very good shot" meaning he could shoot and hit the target. Sure enough there was a little fellow up in a tree. My Daddy shot the gun but did not hit the bear. Knowing he had only one shell, he did not want an angry mama bear to deal with. Where there is a little bear, there is a big mama close by. The bear climbed from the tree and went on his way. We did not eat bear meat that day.

I never was as comfortable in my favorite spot after the intruder was there. My family ate bear meat when it was available. My Daddy often went on a bear hunt with his old buddy Lee Posey. They liked to hunt with dogs. A good bear dog was quiet valuable and their owners were proud! We did not have a bear dog.

To prepare bear meat;

Trim as much fat from the meat as possible. Cut into small one to two-inch chunks. Boil in salted water with a pod of red pepper added. Cook until tender, which meant put the meat on right after breakfast and cook until the evening meal was started. When the meat was tender, remove from the liquid in the pot. Place meat in a baking pan and bake awhile.

To make bear meat and gravy; stir some flour into the broth and pour over the bear meat and bake until the gravy was thick as desired

Sweet potatoes and bear: Cook meat as above, drain off broth. Place sweet potatoes around the edge of the baking pan, pour the bear meat into the middle of the pan and spread to the edge of the sweet potatoes. Bake in the oven until the potatoes are done.

The grease from the bear meat makes the potatoes really good.

Other ways of preparing wild meat

Bear meat can be pressure canned in a mason jar. Trim meat as to cook, pack into the scalded jar up to one inch from the top. Put in one teaspoon of salt, fill with water to come to the top of the meat. Use two-piece lids and tighten. Be sure to wipe the top of jar first. Place in a rack in the pressure canner. Pressure at ten-pound pressure for ninety. Minutes, allow canner to cool naturally.

To serve: Pour broth from meat into a sauce pan add one tablespoon flour and stir, then add the meat cook slowly until gravy is done.

Bar-b-q: drain broth from the meat, place meat in a fry pan, fluff with a fork. Cook until dry then add your favorite bar-b-q sauce and heat. Serve on a bun with a slice of onion and mustard.

Other meats can be fixed the same way, they are ground hog and raccoon.

Other meats that are good canned are beef, pork deer, chicken and tame turkey or wild turkey.

Spice Wood leaves and berries are good to calm the wild taste and add flavor while cooking the meat. Break off a branch, remove leaves and lay over meat. Break branch into smaller pieces and spread over the pan. Best if covered with water. Remove before serving.

Deer have always been in the area. Often times we would see deer when we were walking the road to the store or church. My brother Charles and I were going to the store, we were at the river. All of a sudden we heard an awful commotion, limbs breaking thundering hoofs, dogs barking, a big ten or twelve point buck came with in ten feet of us. We started hollering, the buck turned and went back in the direction of the dog barking. In just a few minutes the deer came off the bank behind us and went into the river. Deer can swim really well. They will usually go to the river every time when being ran after by dogs. Dogs can actually run down a deer and kill it.

Deer meat is the leanest of all meat, and therefore healthier to eat. The back strip is the best part. (The tenderloin).

Slice thin and dredge with flour with salt and black pepper added or seasoning salt added. Fry in hot fat until brown, turn and fry the other side.

Deer steak: cut about three fourth inch thick, marinate in orange juice for a couple of hours. Cook on the grill or roll in flour and fry in a pan of hot fat.

Deer bar-b-q: prepare as for the bear.

Pheasant or grouse: remove the breast and skin, wash in cold water. Roll in flour with salt and b.pepper added. Fry in hot fat.

Wild duck and geese will be tough if the bird is very old. Lots of baking, roasting or pressure-cooking is needed to make the meat tender. For a tender bird: brush with veg. Oil and sprinkle with herbs or spices of choice. Sage, Greek or poultry seasonings are good. Slow roast until golden brown.

Wild turkey, again a tender bird is best or the same process as above is needed. Deep fry turkey strips are good. Roll in flour and fry.

Today the crock-pot is invaluable. Just put the turkey in the pot, on high for a while, then turn on low and cook several hours.

Turkey casserole from crock-pot or canned turkey: Drain off the broth, place turkey (cut into small slices or chunks) in a baking pan. Put two boxes of stovetop stuffing crumbs over the turkey. Mix two cups of broth with two cans of cream of chicken soup and two soup cans of water. Mix well and pour over the turkey and crumbs. Place in the moderate hot oven and heat until bubbling..

Turkey patties: from crock-pot left overs or canned turkey. Chop meat, add one egg, one half cup chopped onion, green peppers and celery (optional). Mix all well; drop by a big spoon onto salted and black peppered flour. Carefully roll in flour and fry in hot grease, turn once. Serve with gravy or heat one can of chicken cream soup.

Fish from the wild

Filet fish or skin and cut into thin slices. Dip in milk and egg mixture roll in cornmeal with a little flour added. Fry in deep fat or hot skillet. Turn only once if frying in skillet.

Trout may be fried whole after scrapping, I prefer to rake a knife over the trout even if no scales are present. Take out the insides and rinse in cold water. Fry as above or stuff with wild rice and nuts, then bake with lemon and black pepper.

To skin a catfish the old time way; Drive a large big headed nail in a tree or post at comfort level. Put a heavy knife blade through the head of the fish and wait a few minutes. Put the fish onto the nail with the color side out, belly to the tree. Cut just behind the head all the way around the fish just barely skin deep. Cut the fins off, pull the skin down in a steady even pull all the way to the tip of the tail. Repeat until all skin is removed. Remove the head and insides. Cut the fish into steaks or slices. Hang the catfish head in an open area a good ways from the house and leave for a year, go back and get the skull, gently pull apart and you will find the crucifix in the skull bone and two dice.

The best way to clean fish is to filet them. Place on a board with a clip to hold the tail. After experienced in filleting you can hold with one hand. Run a sharp thin filet knife along the backbone and down over the ribs, (you can feel the bone). When the first side is removed, do not puncture the insides, lay the slice of fish skin side down and run the knife just beneath the skin and the finished product is a boneless fish filet. Repeat for the other side. Discard the bone and insides intact.

Fish is good baked with lemon pepper or sautéed in butter in a pan or baked in oven.

Place fish on ice as soon as possible when fishing in warm weather, as fish can ruin quickly. If no ice available, remove the insides immediately.

DIGGING POTATOES

The white or Irish potatoes were dug any time in the early fall after the vines turned brown and before the frost starts. The potatoes would chill in the ground if the ground froze. Potatoes would not keep well chilled.

The bushel baskets, pails, buckets, boxes tow sacks and anything else that would hold potatoes, was gathered up and taken to the potato field. A good time to dig potatoes is when the signs are in the legs. Cut potatoes will seal over and not rot. Sometimes the potatoes were dug when the ground was dry, even if the signs weren't right.

Uncle Lloyd would come to our house with his horse and plow and help us dig our potatoes and we would help him. The first trip with the plow was down the middle of the row. Potatoes would fall all over the place. We were stationed at intervals as in the cornfield relay. As soon as the plow went by we would jump into the row and start pilling the potatoes out of the plow's way. Several piles were made below that first row. The plow came back on the side a little ways below the first trip. Potatoes were still falling out of the dirt. The next trip with the plow was on the other side of the row. This might continue for a couple more trips with the plow.

The horse, plow and Uncle Lloyd would move to the next row above where he had just plowed. Right through the middle again. Potatoes came rolling out of the ground. That was a beautiful sight. This time the potatoes were piled in the row below that had already been plowed. The rotation continued until all the rows were plowed. The work did not stop there. Uncle Lloyd would rest the horse for a little while. The whole family was involved in the potatoes digging. The cut potatoes that had been cut with the plow were piled separate from the others. The very small potatoes were piled separate. The other potatoes were put into the containers.

If Uncle Lloyd had brought the sled the potatoes were placed in the containers and placed in the sled. Uncle Lloyd took the potatoes to the root cellar. Some of the crew went to pile the potatoes into the root cellar. The rest of us continued to separate the potatoes into their rightful piles.

The cut potatoes were used up first so as not to waste any. The little potatoes were cooked with the jackets on (unpeeled). In later years I canned the little potatoes and still do today.

We usually tried to make about twenty bushel of potatoes. If the crop was shorter, we used fewer potatoes. If the crop was increased, we used more potatoes. The potatoes could be cooked in so many ways. It was a very stable food.

There were mashed potatoes, where the potatoes were peeled and boiled in salty water until very tender. The water was drained off and the potatoes were mashed by using what was called a potato masher. A hand held apparatus. A big wooden handle was attached to a sturdy metal wire in a zigzag pattern. You held the masher in one hand and moved it up and down and all around in the pan. A little milk or cream was added. A big glob of fresh cow butter was added along with black pepper.

Our family favorite was fried potatoes with milk gravy poured over the top. Peel the potatoes and slice any way you want to. Heat some grease, bacon preferred, in a cast-iron skillet. Add potatoes and cover for the first little while. Turn the potatoes over and cook uncovered until brown. Onions may be added when the potatoes were turned for firm onions. Add onions at the same time as potatoes if you want the onions to cook soft and brown along with the potatoes.

One of my favorite ways was to melt a big glob of butter in a baking pan. Pour course salt over the bottom of the pan. Cut the potatoes in the middle long ways. Lay cut side down into the butter. Salt and pepper the top. Place in the oven and bake until crusty brown, that is what we called baked potatoes.

Roasted potatoes were placed in the oven with out peeling and cooked until done. Another way to roast potatoes is to wrap in foil and place in hot ashes at the campfire. Mama roasted potatoes in a cast iron Dutch oven with coals from the wood stove. When camping another way to roast potatoes is to dig a hole in the ground and put a layer of hot coals from the fire into the hole. Add a layer of foiled or unfoiled potatoes. Cover with more hot coals. A lot of practice is needed to assure perfect potatoes every time. Wait, an hour and dig up the potatoes. Potatoes not rolled in foil will have ashes on them. You can also make a mud coating for the potatoes. The mud will bake hard and can be easily chipped off.

When camping, if no dutch oven or you do not want to dig a hole, here is another way to roast potatoes. Place a forked stick in the ground with the fork at the top. Place another one about fourteen inches away from the other one but in a parallel line. Place a straight stick across the other two resting in the fork. Cut a large piece of tin foil. Roll the end over the stick until secure. Bring the foil down on the ground in an L shape. This needed to be close to the fire. Place potatoes on the foil. Rotate often so even cooking can take place. The foil reflects the fire. You can bake fish in this same way, add salt and pepper as desired. Rotate the potatoes or fish so all sides are exposed to the fire. Fish cooks quicker than potatoes.

A favorite left over potatoes use is to make potato cakes. Use whatever amount of left over potatoes you have. Add one or two eggs depending on amount. Add salt and pepper to your taste. Mix eggs well with potatoes. Stir in a half cup to one cup of chopped onion or re-hydrated onion flakes depending on the amount of potatoes used.. Dip one tablespoon of potato mixture into a bowl of flour. Coat well and place in the frying pan with melted butter or hot grease. Flatten with a spatula. Cook until browned on one side and turn over and brown the other side. It is better to turn only once, the patties will tear apart easily.

Potato puffs can be made the same way except work the flour into the potato and egg mixture and drop by spoonfuls into hot deep fat. Cook until brown. Left over creamed corn can be made into corn puffs the same way. These are so good you might just want to make them from fresh potatoes instead of left overs.

French fries are good, but we never really had them when I was growing up. We had a lot of potato soup. My favorite recipe is: Peel three or four large potatoes, cut into little chunks. Place in a large pot with water to cover potatoes and an extra cup of water. Cook until tender. I like to cook two onions in with the potatoes. Add one teaspoon of salt per quart of food. Stir three heaping tablespoon of flour into two cups of cream or milk. Whisk until no lumps remain. Add to cooked potatoes and cook a few minutes longer. Salt and pepper to taste. Cook salt with potatoes but not the black pepper unless you want your sinuses opened up from the pepper steam.

Add lots of butter; serve with corn bread, Mexican corn bread or saltines.

We made our own potato chips by slicing very thin. Have a cast iron skillet very hot and greased. Place one chip at a time to cover bottom of pan. Cook quickly until golden brown. Remove and drain on paper. We drained on brown grocery bags; we did not have paper towels. Another way we made potato chips, but Mama did not approve. We greased the top of the wood stove or cook stove after a good scrubbing with a dry cloth. We placed the chips onto the stove and cooked them. This proved to be pretty messy at times, when the grease started smoking.

Potatoes were added to soups and stews to stretch them. Potatoes could be added to green beans, peas. Chili, hamburger, meatloaf and just about anything else you wanted.

New potatoes are delicious fried in butter. Place whole potatoes in a pan with melted butter. Cover and cook several minutes. Shake the pan to rotate potatoes and continue cooking until browned. No need to parboil.

If I were to have to choose just one vegetable to eat for a long period of time and nothing else it would be the potato.

When I can the little potatoes, I put them in some melted butter and brown before serving. To can potatoes: wash thoroughly. Place into a quart Mason jar up to one inch below top. Add one tsp of salt and pour water over the salt up to cover the potatoes. Process in a pressure canner for thirty minutes. Go by the Ball Blue Book for canning.

I have seen my Mama peel potatoes and save the peelings to plant when we were low on food and especially low on potatoes. You can save your own seed year after year, or we did when growing up.

The story was told of a man on Alarka who sold potatoes to the Farmers Federation. The man lost his pocketknife. The next year the same man bought certified seed from the Farmers Federation and found his very own pocketknife in the sack of potatoes. He had bought his own potatoes back.

Certified seed are potatoes of one kind planted in a field without other kinds of potatoes close by. Different kinds of potatoes will mix if planted close together.

EVE OF JACK FROST

The leaves were all dressed in their brightest colors of, red, gold, orange, yellow, and purple. Brown and colors in-between. There was a chill in the air, Mama said "It is going to frost tonight I smell it in the air." My Mama always did have a knack for predicting the weather. I will take her word right up there with Bob Caldwell today. Mama read the signs and planted by them as well as about everything she did was by the signs, if you planted potatoes when the signs were in the feet, the potatoes would have little toes growing on them at harvest time. The thighs were a good root vegetable planting time. Mama talked to the woolly worm too. If the woolly worm was brown all over it meant a mild winter, if he was black allover it meant a bad winter. If the black was up front an early frost was expected. If the worm had alternating black and brown rings we could expect a trend of cold then warm weather. Never make any kind of pickles when the signs are in the bowels or feet, if so you will have stinky pickles if making pickles from salt.

Other things helped Mama with her predictions. She would mark the calendar when the first Katydid was heard in the daytime, Three months later frost would come. I don't know just what helped with her prediction today, but there was a lot of work to be done before the frost came.

We always planted late beans, corn, cabbage, turnips and acorn squash. My Parents made good use of the entire growing season. My Grandma usually had a hand in the gardening also. The strong and sweet peppers were still producing. "Tommie-toe tomatoes" were abundant, scattered all over the garden. We picked all of them before frost. We also picked all the green, ripe and in-between big tomatoes The ripe ones were eaten raw, the green ones made into Green Tomato Pickles. Some of the green tomatoes were also rolled in brown paper sacks and kept for several weeks, (not as good but still eatable). Others were sliced, rolled in ground corn meal and fried in hot grease with a little salt and pepper to taste.

Green Tomato Relish

To make relish you would need: 6 quarts of green tomatoes (quartered) 3 quarts small onions (peeled and quartered) 1 quart sweet green peppers (chopped) 1 quart sweet red pepper (chopped). 1 or 2 pod strong pepper (chopped). 3 tablespoons pickling salt. 8

cups sugar, 4 cups cider vinegar, 4 cups water. When using vinegar to aid in pickling, you do not need to observe the signs. In a large heavy kettle place all the above. Cook gently, stirring occasionally, until onions are clear. Pack into hot sterilized Mason jars. Place a two-piece lid and tighten. Boil in a "water bath" for five minutes with a lid on the canner. Allow to cool before removing the canner lid. Makes 12 pints

Chow-Chow

Chow-chow was another way to use up the last of the garden produce. You would need; 2 qts. Chopped cabbage, 4 cups chopped onions, 4 cups chopped green tomatoes, 4 cups chopped green peppers, 4 cups chopped red sweet peppers, 6 tablespoons canning salt, 5 cups vinegar, 3 cups sugar, 4 tsp. dry mustard seeds, 2 tsp. turmeric, 1 tsp ground ginger, 4 tsp. celery seed, and 1 tsp ground mustard. COMBINE CHOPPED VEGETABLES: SPRINKLE WITH SALT. Let stand 4 to 6 hours in a cool place, Drain well. Combine vinegar, sugar and spices; simmer ten minutes, bring to a boil. Pack boiling hot into hot sterilized Mason jars. Tighten two-piece caps. Let seal. Makes 8 pints.

All green and red pepper was either picked or pulled up by the roots and dirt shaken off. Then hung up side down in a dry place. As you can see in the other recipes given, pepper is used in a number of pickles and relishes. Here is a pepper relish.

Pickled Pepper Relish

You would need; 2 each of chopped red and green sweet pepper, 1 ½ cups chopped onions, 2 teaspoons mixed pickling spices, 1 hot red pepper, ¾ cup sugar, 2 teaspoons canning salt, 1 ½ cups vinegar. COVER CHOPPED VEGETABLES WITH BOILING WATER; LET STAND FOR 5 minutes. Drain and repeat the boiling water for 10 minutes. Drain. Tie spices and hot pepper in a cheesecloth bag. Add spice bag, sugar and salt to vinegar; simmer for 15 minutes. Add drained vegetables and simmer for 10 minutes. Remove spice bag. Bring to a rolling boil. Pour boiling hot into sterilized hot mason jars. Adjust two-piece lids, tighten and seal. Makes 6 half-pints.

The cabbage was pulled by the roots, dirt removed and hung up side down in the root cellar. Sauerkraut could be made at a latter date.

All green beans were picked or pulled by the roots. The beans were strung and washed. Some were threaded onto a needle and thread and hung to dry behind the cook stove. These are called leather breeches. To cook, soak in salty water overnight. Discard salty water. Cook in a big pot with a lot of water until tender, fat back makes them better. Other beans were used in making End-of Season Soup and canned. Some of the more mature beans were saved for seed to replant the next year. Mama always canned one hundred quart jars of green beans.

End-of-Season Soup;

Three quarts of peeled quartered ripe tomatoes, one quart sliced okra, one quart whole kernel corn, one quart sliced carrots, one quart peeled sliced white potatoes. And one quart broken green beans. Pour above into a big pot, cook until boiling, and stir frequently. Pour into sterilized hot mason jars. Tighten two piece lid and process in a pressure canner, at 10 lbs of pressure for 90 minutes, or boil in water bath for three hours.

A lot of the drying and canning took place the next couple of days. Not everything could be completed in one day.

The late roasting ears (corn) was cut off at the ground. The whole stalk saved. A double A frame was made with poles and a longer pole connected to the A frames. The poles were secured with bailing wire. The A frames were about as high as the ears of corn grew on the corn stalk. Each stalk was placed along side of the frame, the ears of corn were placed in toward the middle. the top of the corn stalk was bent over the pole. The cornstalks on the other side were bent over the other way .All the ears of corn were placed inside, under the frame away from the frost. It looked like a tent. When we wanted cut off corn we walked under-neath the frame and picked the ears of corn. The corn would keep for several days in this manner. Sweet corn would keep longer than the field corn in the roast ear stage. Other produce could also be stored under the corn frame for a few days such as tomatoes, peppers and green beans. Winter squash, pumpkins, cushaws and potatoes could be kept even longer, until they could be properly taken care of. We kids loved to play under the corn frame too.

The tops of the sweet potatoes were cut off and placed on top of the row to protect from frost if not already dug. After digging sweet potatoes, sort out small ones for canning. Wash and drain pat dry with a towel, spread out on cardboard and place in a warm area to dry. To can small sweet potatoes, boil a pot of water, dip several potatoes into boiling water for a few seconds until skins slip off easily . Repeat until all are done or enough are done to make a run of seven quarts or ten pints. Slip skins and place into hot sterilized mason jars. Make a syrup of two cups sugar and four cups of water, boil until sugar is melted (have hot to pour over potatoes.) Attach two-piece lids and tighten. Process in pressure canner for 90 minutes at ten pounds of pressure. To prepare from jar, pour into a skillet with ½ stick of butter, add some brown sugar and boil until nearly dry. Sweet potatoes will keep dry for many months in a cool place with out any canning. They are good baked, fried or boiled, also can be made into sweet potato pie, candied potatoes and mashed sweet potatoes.

All cucumbers were picked for use raw and pickles.

Bread and butter pickles; two gallon cucumbers sliced, 8 onions sliced, 1 cup salt and one gallon of ice water. Put all above into a big contained and let set for three hours. In a large sauce pan bring to boil; 2 tbs turmeric, 2 tbs allspice, 2 tbs mustard, 1 tbs of celery seed,

5 cups sugar, 5 cups vinegar, simmer for 20 minutes. Add drained cucumbers and pour into a sterilized mason jar. Water bath for ten minutes. Green tomatoes may be substituted for the cucumbers for a delicious pickle. Yellow squash can also be prepared in the same manner.

Zucchini squash is delicious in a jam; Peel large squash close to skin. Scrape out seed and pulp and discard. Cut into small chunks. Boil until tender using a small amt. Of water. Drain. Run squash through a sieve or colander. Use four cups of squash, 2 tbs lemon juice, 5 cups of sugar, and ½ teaspoon of each; ground all spice, ground cinnamon, ground cloves and 1 tsp of butter. Boil on med heat for thirty minutes. Ladle into sterilized mason jars and cap with two-piece lids. Allow to seal, if lids do not seal process in a water bath for ten minutes.

All grapes were picked and either made into jelly or juice. To make an easy grape juice, place 2 cups of picked and washed grapes into a sterilized quart mason jar, add ½ to ¾ cup sugar. Fill with hot water, cap with a two-piece lid and tighten. Process in a water bath for 20 minutes. When ready to use pour juice into a glass leaving grapes in jar. If desired cold chill jar before opening.

As you can see the work continued for several days. This day was bittersweet. The end of the growing season, but the promise of a soon to be much needed rest from all the hard work. The root cellar now held about 1,000 filled quart jars that was my Mothers goal. A big bin of white potatoes, some cabbage hanging from the ceiling. Peppers and onions hanging from a nail in the ceiling and along the walls. Pumpkins and winter squash under the shelves holding the jars. The pumpkins would be used for baking pies and making pumpkin butter, as would the cushaws. Acorn squash would be baked. Cut each in half, remove the seed. Place in a baking pan, trim bottom to sit firmly in pan. Add 1 tbs sugar, same of butter and sprinkle with cinnamon. Bake until tender.

The pumpkin and cushaw butters can follow same recipe as for Zucchini jam, except Cut the pumpkin in half remove seeds and pulp. Bake in a [not to hot] oven until tender. Remove from oven and scoop pumpkin or squash from hull. Run through the sieve and continue as with the zucchini.

We did the same thing year after year. We knew we would be fed through the long cold winter. The food tasted so good. We were so pleased with our summer's work.

Jack Frost did show up that night, covering the mountains and valleys with a white blanket. We had out smarted the ole fellow once again. Maybe I should say my Mama had out smarted him.

THE TOBACCO CROP

The tobacco crop was our only moneymaking crop as I have stated already. There was an allotment given to each tobacco grower. No more than the allotment could be grown. My Daddy was particular with the setting of the tobacco plants. Each row was measured and marked off with a string so as not to set out more than the allotment. This was done after the field was plowed and prepared for planting.

The tobacco plants were grown in a "hot bed" or could be bought from other tobacco growers. My family did both from time to time. A hole was made in the ground for the plants. The plants were set exactly the same distance between each one. A cup of water was poured over the roots of each plant and the plant was settled into the ground with dirt packed around the roots. The whole family was involved in the planting process.

Next came the hoeing and replanting of any plant that had not survived or was looking poorly. We had to keep the weeds out of the patch. Grandma delighted in having us kids pull weeds for the hogs. Suckers were little sprouts growing at the base of the leaves, extracting strength from the leaves. The suckers had to be pulled out; they were easy to get loose. The tobacco leaves were sticky, matting the hair and very hard to wash out. (Old time styling jel).

Topping or cutting the blossom from the top of the tobacco was the next step. All of these procedures helped the tobacco to grow heavier leaves. The leaves were the only part sold.

As the tobacco grew, we primed the bottom leaves from the tobacco. Priming means pulling the bottom leaves from the stalk. We did this by crawling on our hands and knees through the rows. Each leaf was saved and strung onto a stick and saved for drying. A lot of people did not prime the bottom leaves off. The leaves would become heavy and drop onto the ground and rot. That was lost tobacco and lost money.

We were careful to keep the leaves in good shape. Two forked sticks were put in the ground about three or four feet apart. The tobacco stick was placed in the Y of the forked sticks. A string was tied to one end of the stick. A leaf of tobacco was placed on the stick with stem side up. The string was then looped around the stem, and repeated on the other side. When the stick was full, you had two rows of leaves on the stick. The stick was then placed into the tobacco barn to dry. We have dried the leaves in the attic of our house.

Mama kept us collecting the leaves of tobacco any time a leaf turned yellow. We wanted to save every leaf of tobacco. In late August the tobacco was usually ready to start cutting. We sometimes did not have to cut any stalks because we had collected the leaves all the way to the top. If this was not the case, the stalks were cut and the tobacco carried to the barn and nailed to sticks and hung in the barn to dry. The autumn winds helped to dry the tobacco.

The next procedure was to "hand" the tobacco. A "hand" of tobacco was a small bunch of the same colored leaves tied together with a leaf of tobacco. Mama usually did this. She was the best at tying the "hands". We stripped the leaves from the stalk and pilled them into piles according to the colors. There was yellow, brown and red leaves. The red was usually the tips or the tobacco growing at the top of the stalk. The best time to "hand" tobacco was in the early damp mornings or on a rainy day. The tobacco had to be perfectly dry, if too moist it would rot. The tobacco was then placed into tobacco baskets that were big shallow containers made from slats with rounded corners. A blanket or quilt was placed over the tobacco baskets to prevent being dried more or allowing no more moisture to get into the tobacco. When all the tobacco was completed the baskets were hauled to Asheville to the tobacco sales around the first of December.

There were tobacco sharks at the warehouse that would check over your baskets, pull out a bunch of tobacco and if they liked what they saw, they would offer you a cash price for your tobacco. You had the option of selling or allowing your tobacco to be bid off at the sale. It was faster to get the money by selling to the sharks. The chances were better of getting a higher price by waiting for the bidding, the sharks were making money for them self's in this manner. Occasionally selling to them brought a higher price. It was a gamble. We always waited for the sale and received our check in the mail about ten days later

The day the check arrived by mail was a happy event. There were times when we received less money per pound of tobacco than we had hoped for. There was nothing you could do about that. Our creditors were happy to be paid the debt that was owed to them.

FEED SACKS

In mid-December the tobacco check arrived in the mail, excitement was at an all-time high for us and for our creditors. The little country grocery store in our community was owned and operated by Ralph and Dessie Breedlove. They were the kindest of people. We often owed them as much as fifty to sixty dollars. That isn't a lot of money now, but fifty years ago it was a lot of money. The other place where we bought feed on credit was from Kings Feed and Grocery at Lauada. The store was owned and operated by Hill and Vesta King. Both storeowners received the money owed to them before any money was spent on other things.

My Parents always bought a truckload of feed with money from the tobacco check. Tobacco was our only moneymaking crop. Their son Henry would deliver to our house a truckload of Cattle Feed called Sweet Feed and Hog Feed called Shorts. The feed came in cotton sacks. The Sweet feed came in pretty calico and gingham checks.

206

By buying a truckload of feed, there would likely be two or three feed sacks exactly alike. Mama would usually pick the colors of her choice to be used to make dresses for the girls and women. Men and boys shirts were also made of feed sacks if the fabric design was appropriate.

The Shorts came in white cotton, these sacks were used to make under garments, sheets for the bed, dish towels. The Shorts sacks had to be boiled to remove the big bold red letters stamped on the outside of the sack. Not always did the letters come off with boiling. We might have a pair of underwear with letters on them.

The truck would arrive with the feed, driven by Henry with Johnny and Eugene (Gene) to help unload the feed. My Daddy and Brothers helped to put the feed into the side feed room. The truckload of feed would supply feed to our cattle and hogs thought the winter. We usually only had one sow hog, the others were butchered the day after Thanksgiving.

We were allowed to play on the pile of feed for a while. Jumping from one to the other was fun. We each picked out the sack we wanted for our garment and waited for the day to arrive when the sack was empty, washed and ready to be sown. We were as proud as if the cloth had come from Sears and Roebuck catalogue.

SPOOKY TALES

Halloween was a fun time of the year. We did not really go trick-or-treating as kids do now. We did have fun, only if Halloween came on a weekend. We would usually have a bon fire at Emma's house. My Aunt Edna was just a kid at heart and to this day still is the same. She loved to do things with us kids.

We would roast some hot dogs on a stick held over the fire. We would eat and then get our garb on. This usually consisted of a stocking pulled down over our face and tied in a knot on top of our head. Some times we would put a toboggan on our head. Some one might wear a wig, and another tie a bandana over the nose and mouth. Nothing elaborate. Most people went to bed early back then. We knew which of the neighbors stayed up late. The most favorite place to go was Mr. Author Breedlove's house. Mr. Author would be sitting in the chair listening to the radio. Mrs. Sarah would be puttering around in the kitchen. She usually kept cookies made and in a big glass cookie container.

This particular night we were a little late getting started. It started to get dark around five thirty in the evening. When we got to the Breedlove's house, we knocked on the door. Author came to the door. He looked at us; there was about seven or eight of us. He kind of acted funny. He didn't say come in like he usually did. Finally he said "now what do we have here". Some body finally said "trick or treat". Author said, "Oh is that what night it is. I forgot all about Halloween. Well now let me see, I don't have anything to give you youngans. I tell you what, you all go on in the house and I will be back in there shortly." Mrs. Sarah had to give every one a hug. She gave the best hugs. She would ask each a question; of course she was trying to figure out who was who. She knew our voices. Mrs. Sarah would say "Oh my now just look at you. You have grown so much since the last time that I saw you. How is your Mama and Daddy doing? How is the rest of the family?" What grade of school are you in now?" By the time that Mr. Author got back into the house, Mrs. Sarah had every one figured out.

Mr. Author brought in a big tub of home grown apples. Red delicious, Winesap and other varieties. He sat the apples down in the middle of the floor. He and Mrs. Sarah rounded up a chair for every one. We had to take off our disguise and coats and "sit a spell". For once Mrs. Sarah was out of homemade cookies.

Mr. Author went into telling us a story of when he was young. He told one story after the other. We ate apples the whole while. When we started to leave Mr. Author gave each of us a quarter. You may not think a quarter was worth much. Well back then we could get a coke and a candy bar and have money left over for the same another time. Candy bars were five cents each and a coke was seven cents. He had given us a real treat. Mr. And Mrs. Breedlove loved for kids to come visit them. Mr. Author was out visiting in the neighbor hood a lot. Mrs. Sarah stayed at home most of the time. Mr. Author gave a lot of babies a silver dollar when they were born. I still have mine.

Walking along the road someone would tell a ghost story and get us scared. We girls would all huddle together; you know there is power in numbers. The boys would go on ahead and hide, then jump out and scare us. I guess the worst I was scared while growing up was when my two brothers hid in the bus house and jumped out on me. I was walking with the Winchester Girls. I was left to walk alone at their drive. There was no moon that night and I did not have a flash light. I was already scared. The boys had gone on ahead of me. I nearly had heart failure when they jumped out.

We would make it back to Aunt Edna's and stay awhile. We still had to walk back to our house which was over a mile away. After all the spooky stories we had heard it was kind of scary. I made sure to stay close by my brothers on the walk home after the other scare.

HOME-MADE HAIR ROLLERS

When I was growing up, curls were the hottest hair fashion. My hair was straight as a stick and very fine. All of the girls wore curls. They curled their hair and some even went to the beauty shop for a perm. I had never been inside a beauty shop. I was in the seventh grade. I wanted curls. We had no curlers in the house. Mama had a few "bobby pins" but not enough to curl my hair.

Mama knew just how to make home-made rollers. She must have wanted curls too at some earlier time. Mama collected several empty Prince Albert tobacco cans. The slim ones that fit inside a mans shirt pocket. The wire cutting scissors and some heavy duty brown paper bags. Most stores used to put items into brown paper bags, no plastic bags back then. We had never heard the word recycle but anything that could be used to make something else was saved. More things were recycled in the home then.

Daddy helped cut the cans apart into a somewhat flat piece of tin. Mama skillfully cut the tin into strips about one half inch wide and five inches long. The cutting was very tricky because the tin was very sharp and would cut the skin as quickly as a knife. It took a long time to cut twenty-four strips of tin. I cut the brown paper into strips three inches wide and seven inches long. I placed a tin strip on the paper one inch from the edges. I rolled the paper around the tin and folded the edges of paper over. I had a padded wire roller ready for use. I positioned the roller in my hair and wound up a wisp of hair. I then bent the edges over. It worked. We completed the rest of the rollers. Mama got a glass of water and a comb. She carefully wound each roller onto a wisp of hair. I looked funny but when my head touched the pillow it was not funny. The rollers hurt my head. I was determined to wear curls to school so I left the rollers in my hair.

The next morning I found a few rollers in my bed, not a good sign. I removed the remaining rollers from my hair. I had some curls and some straight strands of hair. I went to school with my new "do". I received some looks from classmates. Some of the boys were just plain rude. That night we rolled my hair up on the rollers again. This time I tied a bandana (Aunt Jemima fashion) over my rollers. I still did not get much sleep. There were no rollers in my bed the next morning. I had curly hair. Not nice even curls but they were curls. I finally learned to roll my own hair and sleep with the rollers in my head.

I bought store rollers when I got money. Those things were just as uncomfortable as the home-made ones. If you had curls you had to suffer with the rollers.

HAYSTACKS

My Uncle Lloyd and Aunt Edna had a grass field across from their house called "the meadow' the hay was usually cut twice a year, sometimes three times. The most hay was collected from the first cutting.

My Uncle Everett Wikle who had a mowing machine pulled by horse cut the hay. The mowing machine was the new "machine", not the old sling blade. This machine had two big wheels with a seat in the middle to sit on. There was a blade about six feet long with saw like teeth that cut the hay. A lever on the right side with a handle allowed you to control the blade. The handle could be pulled back to lift the blade to keep from mowing over a rock or other unwanted items. We all thought that new machine was the very "stuff"

The mowing was started at the outer edge of the hay field and made a circle around the hay field. This cut about a six-foot strip. The next round cut just inside the first one, and continued around as before.

The mowing continued in this manner until the entire field was cut. The hay was left to dry for a day or two.

The hay rake, which was the newer way to turn and roll hay. The pitchfork was now used a lot less. The rake was similar to the mower, except there were half moon prongs about three or four inches apart. That kept the hay from coming through the prongs, they were too close together. The hay rake rolled the hay into a pile and continued the pile the length of the row. This made a row of rolled hay about every ten to twelve feet apart.

The hay was carried by a pitchfork and loaded into a horse drawn sled or carried to the haystack. A pole about fifteen or sixteen feet long was "stuck" into the ground and tamped around to make it secure. That pole was called a stack pole. Dry wooden boards were laid on the ground before starting the hay. The hay was packed in a circle around the pole with an eight to twelve foot diameter using from four to six feet radius.

Uncle Lloyd, my Daddy, Calvin Wikle and Uncle Everett helped in the hay. Uncle Everett had hay to cut too. They helped each other. That was called bartering. We kids were allowed to bounce up and down on the hay to pack it down. The men kept coming with more pitchforks of hay and placing the hay around the stack pole. The radius dropped back slightly in order to make a slanting stack of hay. We climbed upon the hay and slid down, then back up again. We thought we were just being given the privilege of playing on the haystack. That was not the case. What we were actually doing was smoothing the hay so when the rain came, the water would slide off over the sides and not go down into the hay and rot. When the stack was as high as desired or when the hay was used up a 'cap' was placed on the stack. To make the cap a big hand full of hay was gathered up in the hand. The hay was wound around the top of the stack pole very tightly and secured with bailing wire or twine. This cap would keep the water from running down the stack pole and rot the hay from underneath.

The first cutting of hay went into the barn either loose or in bails. The last cutting was stacked on the stack poles. The hay field usually yielded about three or four stacks.

We have stored pumpkins under the haystack to prevent them from freezing. The hay cutting and stacking was hot sticky work. The grass dried and the edges were sharp and prickly. It caused the skin to itch. A dip in the creek was very much appreciated. Most times the cows were turned into the hay field after the last cutting took place. They would eat up all the left behind hay, the trampled hay and cow manure helped to fertilize the field for next year.

Sitting on top of that hay stack just waiting to slid down sort of gave one a feeling comparable to being on top a high sliding board on the school play ground.

There is nothing more country smelling than the scent of freshly cut hay.

SECTION SEVEN: WINTER

HOG BUTCHERING DAY

It was actually called hog killing day, but I prefer to call it butchering day. Hog butchering day was a family affair, maybe even a community activity. Several men would help each other with the task. My family usually butchered at least one and sometimes more very large fat hogs. My family raised pigs for sale, as well as food for the family. We never bought meat at the grocery store. We actually didn't buy much at the store. We grew most of the food we ate. Coffee and sugar was about it.

Usually the day after Thanksgiving was the BIG DAY. The day before, we had to get everything ready. A 55-gallon barrel was cleaned and filled to the top with water. This was my chore, carry all the water. My brothers had to gather up a big load of dry wood to go with the green wood that my Daddy cut to make a fire under the water, to heat the water to boiling. The chore of using the boiling water was a job for the men. I am going to leave off describing that task and tell how I was involved in the ---Big Day event.

I had to help my Mother and Grandmother clean all the big kettles, dishpans, pots and frying pans, canners and sausage grinder. We also had to gather up mason canning jars and wash them. This took a lot of water, as we didn't have running water in the kitchen, I had to carry lots of water. We had a reservoir on the side of the wood-burning cook stove, as the food cooked the water got hot.

Bright and early on Friday morning, we were all up early. Daddy built a fire in the cook stove and built a fire under the big barrel of water, Mama cooked a big breakfast. We washed the dishes, cleared the table, and waited for our part to begin. The first thing I had to do was take a big load of the pots and pans to where the men were in the first or second, or third stage of preparing the unfortunate swine for human consumption. There were several more things that needed to be done, which were the women's jobs, I will tell you that no part of the porker went to waste. The fat was saved for rendering into lard. The liver made liver mush. The tail, ears, feet and head were all used. The bladder was cleaned and filled with human air to be dried and made into a ball for all of us five kids to play with.

The hams were "salted down" along with the streaked part of the middle, which was used for bacon (we didn't call it bacon, we called it "fat back".) The back strip was made into tenderloin, backbones and ribs. (If you had pork chops you could not have the tenderloin).

The tenderloin was the first meat cooked. It was usually cooked for lunch along with some hot biscuits, red eye gravy and milk gravy. Fried potatoes and eggs, with milk to drink completed the meal. (Usually enough for about a dozen people.) We had to fill up a plate and go to the living room, because the kitchen table was in use, holding the pots and pans of meat.

The sausage making task started next, while Mama and Grandma cut the meat into strips I did the dishes. My little sisters had to help, which usually took longer but got them out of the way of Mama and Grandma. The old hand turned sausage grinder was securely mounted on the kitchen table. We were all eager to give it a few turns. We soon complained of aching hands and arms. Mama and my brothers completed the endless (or seemed endless) task. When a big dishpan was full, mama would pour in the red pepper, salt, black pepper and the wonderful smelling sage. She always knew just the right amount to make the sausage taste good. No measuring spoons or cups just pinched it up with her fingers or poured into her hand. Next came the mixing the spices into the ground meat, it felt greasy in my fingers. (I forgot to tell you that the men had long ago gone to the next house to skillfully perform the same act of unkindness to the unaware fat hog.). The spiced ground pork was ready to be made into ping-pong ball size sausages. These had to be perfectly round. We were all encouraged to master the fine art of sausage ball making. More often than not Mama had to add her special touch to achieve the ping-pong ball look. Very gently the sausage was placed

Bonnie Lou Cochran

into a large cast iron skillet or baking pan and either fried or baked to a crispy brown. The aroma of the frying sausage was the most wonderful smell in the world. The sausage was gently spooned into a hot, dry canning jar. The hot grease was poured into the same jar; a lid put in place and tightened. The jar was then inverted onto an area prepared away from the "draft", with a heavy towel underneath the jar and another one to cover the jars. If the jar lid did not seal the grease formed a seal and the sausage would not spoil. These unsealed jars were used first.

Usually by the end of the first day all the sausage was made and canned. The evening meal usually consisted of a pot of pinto beans that had been simmering on the back of the wood stove all evening. We were usually not very hungry because we had consumed about a pound of sausage each, right from the pan. A big cast iron pan of corn bread cooked in the oven along side a pan of sausage. Any one not full of sausage could of course have plenty to go with the beans and cornbread. By the time the supper dishes were washed and the kitchen floor mopped it was bedtime. No one complained about going to bed.

The second day, there was still a lot of work to be done. All the fat had to be rendered out. This was a dangerous job, due to the grease popping out of the pans and burning you. The clear hot grease was poured into more canning jars and covered with a lid. The grease would turn a snow white when cooled. This was our "Crisco" to be used for frying and making biscuits for the next year. The remains of the fluffy white fat chunks, after cooking, were little rolled up pieces called cracklens. The cracklens were used to make pork skin snacks and cracklen corn bread. Yummy but probably not on the (good for you) food list of today..

By the end of the second day most of the meat was processed. The supper was backbones and ribs, which had been cooking slowly all day, a big pot of boiled potatoes, corn bread and milk. By this time the entire kitchen floor was covered with a thin (thick in some places) coat of grease. It was a perfect place to practice sliding to home plate. After the first slide, by the first kid, Mama put a sudden end to the fun. The dishes were done, the kitchen floor mopped with a lot of soap and hot water, yes I had to carry the water. There were still a few items to finish up later, like making the pickled loaf from the jaw meat; I never liked the taste of that. By now we were all sick of the smell of cooking pork. Fried chicken for Sunday dinner the next day seemed like the perfect meal. We were glad we did not have to do this again for at least another year.

My Brother Charles decided, after reading this story that I needed to write more. Here goes.

My Daddy was very particular with hog killing procedures. Only one shot was allowed. My Daddy was a sharp shooter. He did the shooting, one shot in the head. The hog's throat was slit to allow the blood to drain from the body, called bleeding the hog. The hog was then dragged to the scalding board. The hot water that was heating in the big barrel over the fire was used to scald the hair on the hog. The hot water was poured over the hogs back. The hair was removed with a dull knife by scrapping the hair loose. A sharp knife would have cut the skin. The scrapping and hot water was continued until all the hair was off. The feet and legs were done last. The water had to be a certain temperature so as not to "set the hair on the hog".

The hog was then "hung". A stick about 2 & 1/2 feet long was sharpened on each end and placed between the two hind feet of the hog. The sharpened edges pierced through the legs just above the feet. The hog was then hoisted onto a scaffold with a come-a-long pulley.

The belly of the hog was slit from top to bottom. The gutting took place next. The insides were removed by placing the hands around towards the backbone on each side and pulling everything out. Care was taken to keep the liver safe. The heart was also saved. The intestines were pilled into a big washtub, all fat removed and saved for rendering the lard. The head was taken off and placed in a tub for continued cleaning and processing. The front legs and shoulders were detached and either carried to the smoke house or salting room, (same place). Most of the time we made sausage from the shoulders. If the tenderloin was cut out, there were no pork chops. The backbone was cut into chunks and put with the ribs, which were chopped into small chunks. The middle meat was "salted down" meaning salt was spread over the meat and left to cure. The hams were salted and usually were sold after curing.

I think I have covered everything. Each man helping usually took home a "mess" of meat if there was not a hog to be killed at his house that day.

Here are some of the other recipes used in cooking the meat of the hog.

Fried Country Ham (sliced) and Red-eye-gravy

Soak the ham in cold water for a few hours to remove some of the salt taste.

Trim some of the fat from the ham and cut ham into smaller pieces. Discard the trimmed fat. Place a little bacon grease in skillet. Add ham and cook slowly until lightly browned on each side. Remove ham to platter. Heat drippings in pan, when hot pour one cup black coffee into drippings boil one minute and pour over ham or serve from gravy boat.

Chicken Fried Pork Chops or Tenderloin

Heat skillet with bacon grease or lard. Dip chops into flour to cover, add salt and pepper.

Fry in hot grease until brown on one side turn, and repeat.

Pig's feet; My Grandma loved to eat the pigs feet. This is how she cleaned and cooked them. The hoof part was cut off outside by the men. Scald and scrape, the skin would be removed or left on. Wash thoroughly if skin left on. Soak in salt water for a few hours, rinse and boil in a big pot of water. Place on the back of the stove and simmer for hours until meat tender and easily removes from the bones. Salt and pepper to taste.

Head Cheese; For every six pounds of scrap chopped meat add 3 tbs salt 4tsp of black pepper 1 tbs cloves 1 tbs red pepper seed. Cook until tender in a pot of water. Allow to cool. Drain off the water. Cool. Place in a shallow dish and mound with hands packing down firm. When cold slice and fry in hot grease or eat cold on bread.

Bar-B-Q Ribs; Cook ribs in a pot with water to cover until tender. Drain water and place ribs in a baking pan add bar-b-q sauce. Bake until browning stage. Remove and let set a few minutes before serving.

Bar-b-q sauce; two cups of ketchup 1/2 cup brown sugar, one teaspoon of dry mustard powder. ½ cup chopped onion 1/2-cup molasses, one-teaspoon liquid smoke. Simmer while ribs are cooking.

Bar-B-Q pulled pork; Bake pork roasts in oven or crock-pot until very tender. Allow to cool. Pull meat from bones, discarding nearly all of the fat. Place meat in a large cast iron skillet. Pour barbeque sauce over meat and fry fast until some is burned on bottom. Stir meat distributing the burned into the rest. Make sure to heat thoroughly. Serve on buns or as a main meat meal.

Liver mush; Wash the liver and soak in cold water for awhile. Slice and trim all veins from the liver.Wash in cold water. Cut into small chunks and place in a big pot. Cover with cold water and cook until tender. Allow to cool. Mash the liver with a fork or potato masher. Add enough water to make three cups of liver mixture. Bring to a rolling boil. Add three fourths teaspoon of salt ., Slowly in a steady stream add one cup of cornmeal. Stir and cook until thick. Ladle onto a plate and round out smooth. (If more spices are desired add to boiling mixture before adding the cornmeal.) Allow to cool,slice and fry. Keep refrigerated.

RAG MOPS AND BROOMCORN BROOMS

We did not have money to go to the store and buy mops and brooms, we made our own. There was a rag box kept to place scraps suitable for mop making. The rags could not be "worn out" meaning they had to be of good strong cotton fabric. The mop was made only once a year. Feed of all sorts came in cotton cloth sacks. Dairy feed usually came in prints. Those were used for shirt or dressmaking Others were used for many things, those that did not have a specific use were used in making the mop. The strips had to be about eighteen inches long. The width did not matter.

Long before recycling bins were introduced the recycling of almost everything took place at our house. If a garment was out-grown and no one else could wear it, the buttons were removed and placed into a button box. The button box held dual duties. We kids were allowed to play with the buttons while Mama and Grandma were sewing or mending. We could string them on a thread and needle, thus getting the "feel" of sewing. A prick in the finger with a needle created caution and respect for the needle. We could practice our math by picking all the same colors of buttons and counting them. We made button necklaces. When sewing time was over, all the buttons were placed back into the button box to await future use. Any time a button was missing from a garment, the button box was sure to solve the dilemma.

The fabric of recyclable garments was respectfully separated into several piles. One for mop making, one for the mending pile, another for making other garments for smaller ones. The left overs that were good were put into the quilt making pile. Almost any fabric could be made into some type of quilt "scrap". The well-worn pieces of fabric were used for cleaning rags and various other things.

The mop making fabric was torn into strips about twelve inches from the edge, leaving a six inch strip of fabric intact at the other end, the end to be attached to the mop handle. A big bundle of fabric was needed. Each torn in the same way. Grandma would hold the handle and placing the six inch intact edge of the fabric in one hand and the mop handle in the other hand, she would start winding the fabric onto the stick. She would say, "Hand me another rag." I would pick up one and stretch it out and hand it to her. She carefully placed it on top of the last one. I would need to hold the handle while she smoothed out the fabric. The process continued until the mop was "just right". I held the handle while Grandma placed the wire. She started the first end of the wire at the beginning of the fabric allowing four inches of the wire to go straight down the fabric, She then started winding the wire very tightly around the stick and fabric, I'm holding the stick. She pulls the wire even tighter with a pair of wire pliers. This continues for three inches down the stick. She now has a one-inch piece of wire sticking out from beneath the wound wire. Grandma cuts the other end of wire about an inch longer and connects the two wires together with the pliers and tightens by twisting the wires around and around each other, then tucks the wires into the mop fabric. We now have a "brand new rag mop" The rag mop served us well.

The broom making was along the same lines as mop making to an extent. We grew our own broomcorn in the garden or cornfield. Broomcorn was very different from regular corn. There were no ears of corn, just stalks. The ends of the stalks grew into a fan shape at the top. The seeds grew like grass seeds all over the top of the stalk. When the corn was mature, Grandma would cut the stalks off at about four feet from the top. The seeds had to be removed. This was done by laying the stalks on the ground and raking a hoe over the ends, which we kids did. Grandma used a big butcher knife to finish scraping the seed off the stalks. The ends were carefully cut from each stalk in a straight line using a pair of sharp shears. The stalk was trimmed to about thirty inches from end to end.

Water would be boiling in the big black pot in the back yard. Grandma used that pot for many things. She submerged each stalk of broomcorn into the boiling water. She waited several seconds, removed the stalks to a screen frame to drip before using. The boiling water softened the stalk and broom straws, the end of the stalk was called straws after the seeds were removed. All stalks were put into the hot water bath and left to drip. Meantime Grandma gathered all the necessary equipment to complete the broom. A large board was place over the backs of two straight chairs to hold the damp stalks. A pair of wire pliers, hammer and a strong wire was placed in reach of Grandma. An old broom was usually torn apart and the stick was saved for this occasion.

Grandma commenced putting the broom together. My help was needed. With broomstick in hand Grandma would say, "Hand me a stalk of broomcorn". I handed her a stalk. She carefully placed it onto the stick about eight inches from the end of the stick,"now gimme another one." Holding very tightly the stick and other stalk, she would put the next stalk into place. This routine kept up until the broom was the size she wanted. She would say, "Now hold this stick and don't let go. Hold it right cher", meaning to hold the corn stalks and the handle very tightly. A wire was started the same as for the mop. Grandma carefully wound the wire onto the broomstick using the wire pliers to help tighten. The wire was twisted together at the ends and tucked into the broom, or if the wire was too stiff to tuck, she would leave the ends out. If this happened she would cut the wire back a little (shorten).

The upper end of the broom stalks were cut slanted at the top above the wire so as to not be so bulky. The broom completed, it was laid on the screen frame to dry completely. The new broom was tried out by Grandma. She swept the floor first using her new broom. Sometimes she would say, "It is a little heavy but will do". The other broom now became the "old broom" and was used to sweep the yard. Some times the broom would be so heavy that a strong woman was needed to use it.

The smaller stalks of broomcorn were used to make a Wisk to remove the corn silks from ears of corn. The seeds were saved to replant the following year. Cakes, pies, and breads were tested for doneness by sticking a broom straw into the center. If the broom straw came out clean, the cake was done.

Mops and brooms were made on separate days due to the harsh twisting of the wire made the wrist sore for a few days.

Grandma took great pride in her work. She did not allow any one to abuse the broom. If she saw someone leaning too hard on the broom while sweeping she would say "quit yer leaning on that broom, them thangs are hard to make."

BLACK POT HOMINY

The big black cast iron pot had many uses. One being to make lye hominy from dried corn. This is a very old recipe handed down to my mother and to me and my brothers and sisters.

The corn needs to be very dry, shucked, silked and shelled from the cob. This shelling usually took place on the night before hominy making.

To make the skin come from the corn some form of lye was used. My parents always used Hickory ashes. The wood was burned in the wood-burning cook stove or heater. No other wood was used with the Hickory. The ashes were collected from the ash box and sifted through a wire sieve. Two cups of ashes were placed into a muslin sack and tied with a cotton thread.

There are two ways to get the lye from the ashes, First method was to pour boiling water over the ashes and leave or steep for a few minutes. The water was then used in the black pot. This way seems nice, but there is no way to determine the amount of lye that will remain in the water after the bag is removed. Only very skillful hominy makers use this method. The other method was to place the sack of ashes in the big pot with four or five quarts of the dried corn. Add cold water to fill the pot nearly full. The fire was then built under the pot. The corn was heated to the boiling stage, full rolling boil. Green wood was then added to slow the heat source down. The corn was boiled until the skins started to slip from the corn. The ash bag was removed. The corn was dipped from the pot and place into clean fresh water and washed by hand. This was repeated for three washings. This removed the skins and hearts from the corn.

The pot was removed from the fire, washed and clean water added. The corn was then placed back into the pot and returned to the fire. This usually took my Grandma and my Daddy both. The corn was stirred with a long wooden stick with a wide bottom. The stick was carved by hand. The corn continued to cook until as tender as one wished. My grandma would dip up a few kernels every so often and taste. When just right, she would stop the cooking process.

The corn was now called hominy. The hominy was fried in grease where fatback pork had been fried. Salt and pepper to suit your taste, or the hominy would be eaten with out frying. The hominy could also be placed in a pan with a little butter and a little water and steamed. Hominy not used right away was canned in Mason jars and sealed.

To can hominy, fill clean scalded Mason jars to with-in one inch of the top. One teaspoon of salt was added. Hot water added to cover the hominy. A 2-piece lid was used. The jars were placed in a canner with hot water to cover up to the shoulders of the jars. Bring the water to a full rolling boil and boil for fifteen minutes.

TODAY'S CROCK-POT HOMINY

Today's crock-pot method of making hominy.

Baking soda is used instead of the lye ashes. Prepare four cups of corn the same as described before. Place the corn into a large crock-pot, dissolve two tablespoons of baking soda in a cup of warn water pour over the corn. Fill the pot nearly full with cold water. Heat on high until a full rolling boil. Gradually reduce the heat, be sure to keep the corn boiling. Cook until the skin turns loose from the corn. Remove the corn from the crock-pot and place into cold water. Wash the corn several times in clean water with each washing. Clean the crock-pot and place the corn back in the pot. Heat on high until boiling. Turn to low and cook for a few hours, stir and taste at intervals until desired tenderness. Fry in bacon grease or butter, Salt and pepper to taste. Be sure to reduce corn if you are using a smaller crock pot. The kernels absorb the water and become much larger than when dry.

LYE SOAP

My Grandma Pearl made all of the soap used by our family. Soap making is not a hard thing to do if you follow the directions exactly. The amount of lye used is the most important item in the soap-making recipe. The most common name brand of lye is the RED DEVIL LYE. The chemical names used for lye is caustic soda or sodium hydroxide All soaps use some form of lye.

The very old timers or pioneers did not have the use of Red Devil Lye. They had to make their own lye from ashes collected from burning hardwood such as Hickory. The ashes were placed in a muslin sack and soused up and down in a pot of water for several minutes. The exact amount of lye was unknown, therefore resulting in hit or miss results. One had to have a lot of practice and patience to get a good batch of soap. One of the ways to test the lye water was to put a finger in the water and taste. This is not recommended. Yet I do know the taste of lye and can usually determine if there is enough lye to make soap lather.

My Grandma used the Red Devil Lye methods for her soap making when I was a child. Full moon is best time to make soap. Soap was made outside on a clear day. The mixing of lye and water causes a toxic fume to rise very quickly. Take care not to inhale the fumes. My Grandma usually used a two-day method. Ten pounds of freshly rendered hog lard was mixed with two quarts of soft water. (Soft water is rain water, water from a well or boiled water). Grandma usually heated the mixture in the Big Black Cast Iron Pot. The mixture was brought to a boil, the pot was removed from the fire or the fire was removed from under the pot. This mixture was allowed to cool overnight. (Hog fat was heated in a big pot on the stove or the Big Black Pot. This fat was called lard after the cooking process. Soap making took place after the hog was killed and the hog fat was rendered. Store bought lard can be used).

Day two, mix together 4 tablespoons white sugar, 6 tablespoons Borax powder, 2 tablespoons of salt, ½ cup of liquid ammonia and 1 cup of soft water. Set aside. Outside In a stainless steel pot pour 2 quarts of cold soft water; slowly add 2 cups of Red Devil Lye. This mixture reacts very quickly, do not breathe the fumes. Turn head to one side and stir with a wooden spoon until the lye is dissolved. Leave mixture to cool to lukewarm.

Put all the lard mixture and the ammonia mixture into the lye mixture and stir gently and completely until thick and creamy. Use a slotted wooden spoon. This may take some time, just keep stirring. When creamy and very thick pour into a greased wooden box or line box with a greased cloth. When set cut into bars. Allow to cure for three weeks before using. Makes 60-75 bars.

Reduced Recipe; 2 ½ pounds of lard heated with 1 pint of soft water. Cool overnight.

1-tablespoon sugar, 1 ½ tablespoon Borax powder, ½ tablespoon salt, 1/8 cup of ammonia liquid, ¼ cup soft water. Set aside. Mix 1 pint of soft water with ½ cup lye. Mix all together and gently and completely stir until creamy and thick. Makes about 12-15 bars of soap. This is a good trial size. Soap can be molded in plastic or wooden molds,

(Lye will damage aluminum; use stainless steel.)

To make lye soap less abrasive substitute part of the water with aloe juice. If making baby soap or soap for very sensitive skin substitute all the first water used with aloe juice. (The water used with the lard.)

To add color to lye soap add the dye and mix well just before pouring into the box or mold.

Shampoos using a lot of salt will cause hair loss. Check the labels for sodium.

Additional hair loss is normal for women who have just had a baby.

God made a few perfect heads, the rest he put hair on. Author unknown.

Baldness represents power in men.

THE BAPTIZING HOLE

The Licklog Creek was a lot bolder then than now. The pond below the Hightower Church was the local swimming hole as well as the baptizing hole. It was not real deep but deep enough for kids to play and swim and for adults to get wet without getting their head wet. The water was about waist deep on an adult.

When people were saved at the church they were then submerged into the water of Licklog Creek. My Daddy was saved in the wintertime before Christmas. He wanted to be baptized on Christmas Day. The preacher and deacons had never had a request of that sort before. They agreed to do it.

I want to tell the events leading up to my Daddy accepting Jesus Christ as his Lord and Savior. My Daddy had been fond of drinking and when he did not have the will power to resist the alcohol he would over indulge and be drunk. That did not happen a lot, but it still did happen. My Daddy had been what was called "under conviction for some time". I guess he felt like things were closing in on him. My Mama and others had been praying that my Daddy would get saved. Daddy got to drinking and drank a lot more than he should, He be came delirious, seeing things and a lot of other things. Some of the men from the church came to talk to Daddy. They gave him a lot of strong black coffee and kept him company. The men had been holding prayer meetings on the hillside about once a week. Daddy would go but not get too close for comfort. As Daddy "sobered up" he came to his right mind and decided that he did not want to go on living the way he had been. He wanted to give up the whisky. All the churchmen of the community were praying for Daddy along with my Mama and others.

My Mama had a place in the back bedroom where she often went and got down on her knees to talk to God. I went along with her and got down on my knees too. I did not pray much, but I watched and listened to my Mama pray. This day was no exception; I went with Mama to pray for my Daddy and that he would be saved. Mama got up from her knees and went back into the living room (front room then). I heard Mama tell some of the churchmen that God had revealed to her that Daddy was going to be saved that day. Everyone there had talked and tried to explain the plan of salvation to my Daddy to no avail. Finally one of the men said, "Who do you think it will take to say the right words to Luther". No one would even suggest anyone.

My Mama said "I will go pray again" To the exact spot in the back bedroom as before, my Mama got down on her knees and started talking to God. I was right by her side, I did not want to miss a thing. My Mama talked to God the way she talked to others, as if He was standing in the room looking at her. This is what she said "God you told me that you were going to save Luther today, now God who is it going to take to lead him to you?" I was right there with her, but I did not hear God say anything. My Mother got up from her knees and went back to the living room and told the men "God said it would take "Preacher Martin Cable, does any one know where he might be"?

The men were in conversation trying to figure out where the preacher had gone off to. Preacher Cable was from the area that my Daddy grew up in and all had to move out because the Fontana Dam was built. My Daddy respected the preacher. Preacher Cable often was a traveling minister to other parts of the state. No one knew where to find him.

My Mama again went into the back bedroom and got down on her knees and started praying out loud as always. I was right by her side as always. Mama said "God, You said that Luther was going to get saved today, You said Preacher Martin Cable was the one needed, now God please send Him here."

In the meantime one of the men that had a car (very few cars in the community back then) went to Bryson City to see if he could find

Preacher Cable. Low and behold (a favorite saying when something was out of the ordinary) not long after Mama got through praying, that the man who had the car came driving up our road and stopped at our house. The man who got out of the car with him was none other than Preacher Martin Cable.

Seemed he was out in midstate and decided to go to another town to (Hold a Meet'n). He rode the Trailway Bus to get from town to town if no one offered to give him a ride otherwise. He went into the bus station and told the ticket seller where he was planning to go, and got a ticket to that town, He thought. When the preacher got into the bus, he looked at the ticket, to his surprise the ticket was to Bryson City instead of where he was going.(or thought he was going). When the preacher got off the bus in Bryson City, the man from our community who had the car was driving by the bus station and saw Preacher Cable. He stopped and told of my Daddy's situation. The two men then drove to our house. My Daddy was receptive of the preacher's invitation to accept Jesus as his Lord and Savior. Talk about faith, that was a sure faith builder.

On Christmas morning the weather was very cold. Mush ice was floating in the creek. The church was a short distance from the creek, but far enough away to need a vehicle to take a wet person to the church. The men had built a big fire in the old pot bellied stove in the basement of the church. The room was a Sunday School classroom. The church had no bathroom indoors. Several people met at the church and all congregated to the creek. My Mama had a blanket for my Daddy to wrap up in after getting wet.

My Uncle Wayne Ammons was the song leader. He started up the old hymn: Shall We Gather At The River? Every one joined in with the singing. My Daddy had worn warm clothing complete with long handled underwear.

The creek looked very cold with the mush ice floating. My Daddy did not waiver; He stepped into the icy water along with the preacher and my Uncle Adam Sutton my Daddy's brother. No one let on about the cold water. They situated my Daddy's hands across his chest. The preacher held up his right hand, the other one on my Daddy's arm, and said, "I baptize this my brother Luther Sutton in the name of the Father, Son and Holy Ghost". My Daddy was submerged into the water and back up. The singing, shouting and praising God was all taking place at the same time.

A vehicle was waiting to take my Daddy back up to the church to change clothes. A towel was over his head and a blanket around his shoulders. Some people thought that my Daddy would catch pneumonia, but he did not even get a cold.

That Christmas Day was very different from the others as will be explained later in a different story.

SHORT DAYS AND LONG NIGHTS

Wintertime brought cold north winds, Jack Frost, freezing rain and snowflakes. The chores of getting the wood boxes filled, putting up the chickens, feeding the pig and milking the cow all had to be finished before dark. The darkness set in about five thirty to six o'clock in the evening. We got home from school right around four o'clock. We had to start on the chores right away.

After we got running water (literally running water, there was no way to turn the water off.) Gravity flow brought the water down off the mountain and into the sink by a pipe. The pipe was mounted to the sink but no spigot. That is the way the water still was when I left home in 1967. When a bathroom was added in the room that was mine. (It was only mine after my brother left home in 1964.) Along with the indoor plumbing a spigot for hot and cold water was installed.

My chore changed from carrying water to cooking supper and washing the dishes. My mother was sick with heart trouble. She had good days and bad days. Cooking came easy for me and I loved it. Mama or Grandma would put on a big pot of beans right after we left for school and slow cook them all day on the wood heater in the front room. This room was at the front of the house and the first room you came into when entering the front door. A big chunk of streaked hog meat would be cooking in the pinto beans. Streaked hog meat was the fat belly part of the hog. It would now be bacon. It was called streaked meat or fat back. We usually bought fifty pounds of beans at a time.

If no beans were cooking, mealtime was still easy. We had canned green beans, sour krawt, canned meat, tomatoes and lots of other good things. I just opened one or two cans of two or three things and put them in a separate pot and heated. I baked a cake of corn bread. A cake of corn bread was just a pan of corn bread baked in a cast iron skillet. A cake of bread was biscuit dough made into a thin batter and poured into a greased hot skillet or pan. (Often called batter bread.) My Daddy called it splatter bread and he did not like bread that way for breakfast. He preferred biscuits.

We sometimes had fried potatoes with gravy to pour over them. That was not one of my earlier dishes. If I did potatoes, I usually boiled them and made mashed potatoes, I had to have help with the masher. Fried potatoes were a family favorite and it took a big pan full. We did not have desert for supper much. We did have jams and jellies and canned fruit available by only popping off the canning lid.

One of my favorite potato dishes was creamed potato soup. I still love that dish today.

Our family was not picky like kids are today. We learned to eat and like about everything. We each had our favorites, and I had a lot of favorites.

If a fox or "possum" came around the chicken house the night before, the chickens were hard to get to go to roost in the pen. Most chickens would go to roost early, thus the old saying "He goes to bed with the chickens" meaning He goes to bed early. The chickens would go to roost in the very top of a tall tree. We would get the two flashlights kept in the house and try to find the chickens. We would have to scare the chickens from the trees and chase them into their pen. This could be quiet time consuming as well as getting chilled by the cold night air. There were different ways to get the chickens from the trees. We would shine the light into their eyes, shake the tree limbs, and throw things into the tree. At times nothing worked and we would shut the chicken house door and leave the strays out hoping the fox or "possum" did not catch them before daylight. A"possum" can climb a tree but a fox cannot.

We would be finished with chores, supper and the dishes by about seven or seven thirty. If no chickens went astray we would have some time on our hands before bedtime. Our homework had to be done and then we could play a game. We had no TV and no radio until much later.

My Grandma went to bed at eight thirty every night and Mama and Daddy went to bed at nine o'clock every night of my life, I do believe. We were allowed to stay up to nine thirty or ten depending on our age. Grandma couldn't hear well so we did not disturb her. If we disturbed Mama and Daddy we had to go to bed earlier. We played checkers, Chinese checkers or a home-made board game called Waa-hoo. The game was taught to us by Alvin and Maude Breedlove. We spent many hours playing that game. There is a similar game called "SORRY".

On weekends we did not have to do homework at night. Mama would read to us from a library book. She sometimes would read the Bible to us. We would all pile up on the couch or sit near the heater, depending on how cold it was. The house did not have any insulation so it could be quiet drafty. There have actually been times when snow would blow through the cracks in the walls during a windy snow storm. My Grandma fixed a quart of water to set by her bed each night. She would take her medicine and drink some of the water. Mamy times I have seen the jar of water frozen into ice by morning.

My Daddy worked on his leather crafts or the chains that he made from copper or aluminum, which were used for pocket watch chains and wallet chains. I either inherited my love of making crafts from my Daddy or my Aunt Edna or maybe both. My Daddy took a big nail or peg and wound copper or aluminum wire around the peg from top to bottom. He sawed the wire through with a hack saw. The links were smoothed and one link was pinched together at the edges. The next link was inserted through the first link and pinched together. This continued until the desired chain was the length Daddy wanted. He would trade the chains for something else or just give them to family and friends. My Daddy continued to make his leather crafts until about a year before he died. He designed a wallet with a secret panel. I have never seen a wallet anywhere made the way he made those. He also made regular wallets, belts, gun cases for hand guns and Bible covers. Daddy showed all us kids how to lace leather but I did not master the art of it. Mine was never even like Daddy's were.

I slept in the bed with my Grandma forever, from the time my brother Charles was born when I was 29 months old until my older brother Marvin left home to go to college when I was 16 years old. I then got his old room. We actually only had two bed rooms for a long time. Daddy built a back porch onto the house. He then boxed it in for a dinning room. Later he made an extension to that room and put the kitchen there. A hallway and bedroom was made where the old kitchen had been. After I left home that bedroom was made into a bathroom.

Mama and Grandma would heat a cast iron pressing iron on the wood stove and take to bed wrapped in an old blanket or shirt. The iron was placed at the foot of the bed and gave off warmth to help keep their feet warm The next morning the iron was placed back on the stove and heated during the day to use again the next night. We only had wood floors with linoleum coverings, maybe a crocheted rag rug at the bedside. We left our shoes by the stove to be warm for the next day. By the time I went to bed the bed was toasty warm. Grandma sometimes complained about my cold feet.

We got up at six o'clock or a little after to get ready for school. I never hadto help with the breakfast. Mama and daddy fixed breakfast. My Daddy could cook as well as my Mom could. He made biscuits and gravy, Mama did the other things. The school bus came by our house between seven and fifteen after. The bus had to go up the road and turn around, then come back by our house. We had a few minutes to walk to the road. That was after the bus started to come by our house, before, we had to walk down the road to meet the bus. We got really cold waiting for the bus even with a bus house. (A bus house is a little block building with no door, just a shelter from the rain and snow) The first bus house was a wooden one that was about to fall down, the county built new ones. Riding the school bus was the only way we had to get to school and we were thankful for the bus. My brother Marvin got the job of driving the school bus his last year or so of high school. He had to park the bus up at the Ammons' place. Marvin walked up there each morning and back in the evening.

My Mama and Daddy talked about having to walk to school. There were no snow days for them. We loved when it snowed, that meant we did not have to go to school. My Mama lived close to the Hightower Elementary School and did not have far to walk. My Aunt Edna is two years older than my Mama. Aunt Edna was sick one year and missed a lot of school. She went into the same class the next year. Now there was only one year between their school grades. My Grandpa DeHart did not want Edna to go to Almond High School alone, so he talked the teachers into allowing Edna to go another year at Hightower School. Mama and Edna entered high school the same year and graduated together. Two other families in the neighborhood also had two children graduating the same year as Mama and Edna. I do not know thier reasons.

We did not get a television for a long time. We sometimes walked to the neighbors house to watch a special program.

LESSON LEARNED

Marie Davis and I were friends. She was a year younger than me. I was at her house a lot of times during my childhood. Marie's dad worked as the custodian at the Almond Elementary School for many years. That was when the school was heated with a coal furnace with heat piped through the radiators. I would occasionally go into the boiler room with Marie to see her Dad.

Just below Marie's house between her house and her Grandma Cora Breedlove's house was a big apple tree. The tree was located just below the public road. We walked to church and to visit Aunt Edna and of course we checked under the apple tree for apples each time we passed in the summer.

Cora Breedlove liked children, she was a petite lady with long hair combed back behind her head and fastened in a bun. I never saw her without an apron on over her clothes. She even had a prettier apron for Sunday. There were kids in and out a lot at her house. My favorite thing at her house was her spring house. She had the biggest spring house of all.

It was located underneath a big evergreen tree. It was very cool in the spring house. Cold water ran in a trough the entire length of the house. She kept milk; butter and other foods cool there. I had to have a drink of water every time I went there.

One winter day after a big snowstorm came; we decided to go snow sledding up on the hill above Marie's house. Marie had a brother named Gary. He was the oldest of all us kids. Gary got a bright idea of tying all the three sleds together and all nine of us kids riding down the hill together. The main road went right by their house. On top of the steep bank was a dozed out dirt road going around the side of the hill. We had been stopping in the dirt road with our homemade snow sleds. The more weight on the sled the faster it would travel. We all pilled on after connecting all sleds. We went down the hill very fast, we did not stop as usual. The ones on the front sled yelled "lay down we are going under the fence". I was on the back sled, I rolled off and a couple others did also. The rest went under the barbwire fence down the eight-foot embankment into the main road. We only had a few cuts and scratches, no real injuries, thank God. We did not try that trick again.

Snow Cream was a treat very much looked forward to when the first snow came. The snow needed to be pretty deep. We took a dishpan out to collect the snow. The snow was collected from a clean area, never from the ground. The top of a vehicle or shed were good choices. We took the snow back into the house for Mama to make the fluffy white stuff into a treat.

Snow Cream: Pour clear corn syrup over the snow; add enough cream or milk to mix well. Add vanilla to taste, depending on the amount of snow. Serve immediately in bowls. The snow reduces in size when mixed with the milk. A lot of snow was needed.

Snow cream is still a treat today. I made it for my children growing up.

SNOW VACATION

My Mama used to say "I can smell snow in the air." Mama was a good weather predictor. She used a lot of "signs" to help her. She watched the wooly worms, the chickens, the cattle, the sky, clouds and moon. Today two different factors were involved. The saying "if it clouds up on a frost, snow will fall before dark" was one and Mama's nose the other one.

Daddy spent most of the day getting a big pile of wood for the wood burning cook stove and the heater. Some of the bigger blocks of wood had to be split with a "go devil", a heavy metal tool which had a bottom edge similar to an axe blade. The top part was round and flat. This part was used to hammer on the wedge that was placed in the center of one end of a block of wood. The wedge was held with one hand and the "go devil" handle with the other hand. You drew back and hit the wedge as hard as you could with the "go devil" head. This was repeated until the block of wood started to crack. The axe was used to finish splitting the block into two pieces. The halves could be split the same as the block.

By the time we got home from school Daddy had a huge pile of wood ready to be carried to the front porch. Usually the wood chores were my brothers. Today I was encouraged to get the water carried and help with the wood. Mama said the magic words. "It is going to snow". Excitement was high. After carrying the usual amount of water I started to help with the wood. We carried arm load after arm load to the front porch and stacked it by the side of the house. We continued to stack the wood on both sides of the entrance door. Cook stove wood was carried into the kitchen and put in the wood box. Extra wood was stacked on the back porch for the kitchen stove.

The other chores were completed. The chickens went to roost early, another sign that bad weather was on the way. Just as the last chores were completed a few snow flakes began to fall. Excitement was at an all time high for us kids. Snow meant no school for us. It was early in the week, maybe two or three days out of school. We kept looking out to see the snow flakes falling. The ground was cold, the weather was perfect for the snow to lay and not melt. The question was, "is it laying"? Yes the snow was laying. Big pretty flakes were steadily falling. Soon the ground was white.

After supper, and the dishes were washed, we ventured out into the falling snow. What fun to catch a snow flake on your tongue. We were ordered back into the house by Mama. We had snow in our hair and some on our back. Daddy said "this one may be a doozie". He meant we were probably going to get a big snow.

We didn't even do our homework that night. We played the "wa-hoo board" for what seemed like hours. All of a sudden the electricity went off. We were in the dark. We knew right where the kerosene lamp was kept for just this type of an emergency. We needed light to see how to play the game. My brother soon had the lamp glowing. We were pleased with the light. Finally away up in the night we were instructed by Mama to "go to bed".

The snow continued to fall all night. By morning we had nearly fifteen inches of the beautiful white stuff. Daddy had already been out and measured the snow by the time we got out of bed. Mama had lingered in the bed this morning and allowed us kids to sleep in. We were about an hour later getting breakfast than usual. My brother put on rubber boots and went to feed the hogs and chickens. Milking the cow was done by Mama. Daddy went to help with the feeding. We were anxious to get out in the snow. We didn't have a good pair of rubber boots each. We put on two or three pairs of mismatched socks and borrowed boots from Mama and Grandma. We wrapped our feet in plastic bread bags to keep them dry. We had to bundle up real good with coats, toboggans and gloves. If we didn't have gloves we put socks and more plastic bread bags on our hands. We were instructed by Daddy to shovel a "trail" to the barn, pig pen and chicken house.

We did not have a snow shoved, all we had was a couple of regular shovels that were used for a lot of chores. We cleaned out the barn in the spring and shoveled the manure onto the garden spot. The chicken house and pig pen received the same treatment with the use of the shovel. The shovel was important and had to be treated with respect as did all farming tools. We began shoveling the snow. The snow was heavy and it was hard work to make a path. We took turns with the two shovels, there were three of us shoveling. We went into the house to warm by the stove when we switched shovels.

We stopped for lunch. We talked Mama into making snow cream. It was easy to collect snow, I soon had a dishpan filled. Mama got the other ingredients ready while I gathered the snow. First she poured vanilla flavoring in little dots all over the snow. Next she poured the clear Karo syrup over the top of the snow If Karo syrup wasn't available regular sugar was used. Sugar doesn't dissolve as nicely as the syrup. The syrup also gave a little different taste to the snow cream. Last came the milk and cream. The more cream in the milk the better the snow cream. We had plenty of milk from the cow. Heavy cream came to the top of the jar and the milk stayed below the cream. When Mama poured the milk from the jar the cream came out first. Mama knew just how much to add to the snow. If a little too much milk was added we could collect more snow. It took a lot of snow to make enough snow cream for our family. We each filled a bowl and began to enjoy the wonderful taste of the best snow cream in the world.

The dishpan was soon empty and washed, ready for the next use. I filled the dish pan with snow again and put it on the table. Later the snow was melted and the pan was half full of clean water. The water was poured into the reservoir to be used for dish water. I did that a few times. Later in the evening I still had to go to the spring to get fresh drinking water for the night.

We continued to shovel the snow from every path, including the spring and the out house. We worked really hard that day. We made a big snow man while clearing the paths. We would get a shovel full of snow and roll more snow up with it while clearing a path. We did not want any debre in with the snow for the snow man. We all three worked to get the first big ball of snow just where we wanted to make the snow man. We made a huge round ball by shaping the sides and packing the snow. This was the bottom part of a snowman. We made a smaller ball for the tummy and a much smaller ball for the head. It took all three of us to get the second ball upon the first one. We made the snow man where the girls could look out the window and see him. The rest of the family looked out the window to see the progress of the snowman. Mama worked on her patching. Grandma pieced quilt squares and Daddy worked on leather crafts.

We put an old hat on the snowman's head. He had marble eyes, a wood chip nose and a corncob pipe sticking from his mouth. We gave Mr. Frosty twig arms and stood the old broom beside him. We were very proud. There would be no school tomorrow. The snow had not even started to melt. That night the temperature dropped below freezing.

The next day we took our home-made wooden snow sleds into the pasture. We climbed to the very top of the hill. At first we were not able to move through the snow very well. The snow was too deep for good sled riding. We began working on our route. We pulled the sled up and down until a good slick path was made. We began riding the sleds. The more we packed the snow the faster the sleds traveled down the hill. At the bottom of the hill a little trickle of water spread out six or eight feet making a nice little skating spot when frozen. Today the water was frozen and covered with snow. We usually stopped just before we got to the water. After several trips down the hill we began to go farther and father. Just below the icy spot was an old road. The pasture continued down another little hill with a creek at the bottom.

We kept riding the sleds. The very last trip we were going to make for the day, the sleds went onto the icy spot then shot out over the road and down the other hill. We ended up in a heap in the creek. The parts that were not already wet on our body were now wet. It was time to go to the house and get warm and dry. We gathered around the wood stove in the living room. Little puddles of water were forming at our feet from the melting snow and the water dripping from our clothes. We changed into dry clothes and moped up the water in the floor. We spread our clothes to dry on the backs of chairs beside the stove. We were tired. Mama made us hot cocoa to help get us warmed up.

To make hot cocoa or chocolate; In a sauce pan put one half cup of sugar, one forth cup powdered cocoa, a pinch of salt and one cup of hot water. Boil while stirring constantly for two minutes. Pour in a quart of milk and one half teaspoon vanilla. Heat slowly, do not boil. Double the recipe for a crowd. Our family was a crowd of eight.

The next day the weather was a little warmer. We decided to build an igloo in the front yard. The first thing we did was to remove the snow to make a spot for the igloo. We carried a bucket of water, got the shovel and a tool with a long sharp blade and a handle. The sharp tool was used to whack off excess snow and make the bricks even. We started making snow bricks. The snow had to be packed down, then wet with a little water. As each brick was made it was placed in the proper order. We had a bottom layer in a circle shape, except the entrance way was left open. This was really cold work. We alternated the beginning of each brick just as the picture in our school book showed. We stayed with it as long as we could stand the cold. We couldn't be "running in and out" of the house all the time. We worked for awhile, then rested by the fire for awhile. Then we would go back to the task. By late evening we had the side wall in place.

The next day we started work on the igloo again. It took us most of the day to fix the dome and part of the entry way. The third day we finally had the igloo completed. The entry way was about two feet high and the igloo was about four feet high and about six feet across the middle. All three kids could easily get in the igloo and be fairly comfortable. It was cold inside the little ice house.

We sneaked a little pine kindling, some dry wood and matches into the igloo to make a fire. We sat on boards so as not to get our rear wet. The smoke soon was rising from the pine wood. The warmth from the fire felt good, but the smoke was hovering all around us. We knew not to build too big of a fire as it would melt the roof of the igloo. We felt very proud of our icy domain but decided the warm house was better.

The igloo "kept" for several days. We spent some time playing in the igloo but not as much time as we spent building it. The snow man we built the first day stayed with us a long time too. We finally went back to school after being out for a whole week. What a wonderful "snow vacation".

SECTION EIGHT:
HAPPENINGS

HIGHTOWER BAPTIST CHURCH

Growing up in the Church was sort of like a family reunion every Sunday except no dinner. Occasionally we went to the Maple Springs Baptist Church with Mr. Mose Wikle. But our home church was at Hightower. The Church was a school where my mother attended as a girl. I remember the old school desks being in the class rooms of the church and in the basement. There was a very large room to the left side of the church and just below that room was the basement.

An out side toilet sat up on the hill directly facing the church doors. The person standing in the pulpit could see every one who went to the toilet. No privacy. I mean some toilets were kind of behind the church, not so with this one. Thank heavens for the indoor bathrooms added.

On Sunday morning at 10:00 Sunday School started with singing in the choir, which consisted of most of the people who attended. The song leader was my Uncle Wayne Ammons. The Sunday School superintendent was my Uncle Adam Sutton. I believe my Uncle Adam told me that he served in that position for forty eight years. A very long time.

My Uncle Wayne taught the young peoples class. Mr. Fred Ammons taught the adults. My Aunt Edna sometimes taught the little class.

The Wayne Ammons Family, Fred Ammons family, Vance Winchester Family, Adam Sutton Family, Edna and Emma and sometimes Lloyd Sutton, My family including my parents, my Mama more regular than my Daddy. Florence Breedlove and Family attended until they moved out of the community. Stella Dehart and Family attended until they moved. Author and John Breedlove attended until their death. Everett Wikle and Calvin attended.. Mr.& Mrs. Andy Posey came and brought the girls when they were alive. Other people came at intervals and occasionally others came. Alvin Breedlove Family, and Thurman and Freddie Breedlove Family attended. Over the years people came and went, others stayed, there is no way to name them all.

Preachers that I remember when I was growing up are; Rev. Martin Cable, Rev Tom Pilky, Rev Ed Cook, Rev. Riley Ball (my Daddy's Uncle) and Rev Wendell Crisp. All of these men had families that attended with them. Mr. Gilford Williams came with some of his family and always his musical instrument. He could pick and sing so well, I just wanted the singing to go on forever. There were many others over the years after I left home.

I remember going to people's homes on Wednesday night for prayer meetings instead of meeting in the church. This went on for several years and then Wednesday night services were moved back to the church when the interest slacked off. Usually the homes would be better attended than the church. This was good if a person was homebound and couldn't get out, the service could be held at their home. It was a volunteer rotation. No one was required to host the service.

I have fond memories of the church, even though I attended regularly, I accepted Christ as my savior at the Maple Springs Church at a revival. I was baptized in the Little Tennessee River at the mouth of Wiggins Creek.

There was a cemetery associated with the Church but not owned by the Church. The Windy Gap Cemetery was located about a mile on around the road past the Church. The name of the cemetery has been kind of confusing. Some people called it the Grave Gap. The name up now is Grave Gap Cemetery. The Church is owner of the cemetery at this time, just recently the change was made.

Another change made at the Church several years ago was the addition of a new fellowship hall constructed under the pastorate of Rev. Max Cochran. It is a great asset to the Church and community.

Daddy became a regular member and was very faithful for many years. In February this year, 2004 he died. He was taken to the church on visitation evening and remained in the church all night. Family members and friends stayed the night through with him. His funeral was in the church the next day. My mother still attends the church. My husband and I attend Whittier Church of God now.

OH JOHN

There was no indoor plumbing in the house for many years. There was no running water for several years. Daddy finally got enough water pipe to gravity flow water into the kitchen sink. There was no facet to turn the water off, it was a constant flow, as I said "running water", and we were ticked to have the water piped into the sink, especially me. Carrying the water was my chore.

The "bathroom" was an outside "John", a toilet. A little four-sided house with one side being the door. It was dark inside except for the light coming through under the roof. The sides did not go all the way up to the roof. Some toilets might have a cut out in the shape of a moon or heart or a tiny window. There was a big hole dug out underneath the toilet that was the septic hole. Toilet paper was not a usual item in the household. The mail order catalogues were taken to the toilet to be used as toilet paper.

My Uncle's family had a big toilet, a three seater. They had a large family. The middle seat was small for little kids use.

We got a new toilet built, we thought we were upgrading by having the toilet over the creek like most of our neighbors. No one in the neighborhood had indoor plumbing. The first family to get a bathroom in the house was Jessie and Grace Davis, parents of my friend Marie. I was very fascinated with the new addition to their house.

While we were living by the river our toilet was built on the riverbank-extending out over the river far enough to catch the current. There had been a lot of heavy rains recently. I was small, I remember looking down into the swirling river currant and thinking how big the river had become. I just came out of the toilet and had not even gotten back across the road when the engorged river lifted our toilet off the anchored poles and carried it swiftly away. Only minutes before I was in that toilet. God was surely watching over me that day.

My family put a bathroom in my bedroom after I was through high school and gone from home.

As I take a shower now I often thank God for indoor plumbing and a hot water shower. The only way we had to take a bath was in the old washtub, or with a pan of water and washcloth. Then it was just once a week. We washed our hair in the kitchen sick under the cold running water or poured warm water over our heads from the teakettle. There were times when we were just plain dirty when going to school. Other kids told us we were dirty.

Our only toothpaste was baking soda. Store bought tooth brushes were rare. Birch twigs were often the only tooth brush available to us. My Grandma went into the hospital from time to time, we took turns getting the new tooth brush that was given to the patients at the hospital. The little tube of toothpaste was shared by all.

THE SABBATH

The Sabbath being Sunday was a much-anticipated day of rest. We knew there would be no extra chores to be done like working in the fields or garden. The usual milking and feeding of the animals of course had to be done on Sunday same as any other day. We got out of bed about the same time as every other day. When daylight came, it was time to be out of the bed. We never had an alarm clock. We kept an old rooster who crowed every morning very early. He would continue crowing for some time. It was difficult to sleep with him doing his duty.

Sunday morning breakfast was no different, except Mama might make chocolate gravy and hot biscuits instead of the milk gravy. That was a special treat. After the dishes were washed and put away, the floors were swept and the house got into "order" because some one might come visiting this day. We dressed in our best clothes, called Sunday best or Sunday –go-to-meeting clothes. We didn't have many clothes, usually hand-me=downs or ones made from a flour sack. We wore the same clothes each Sunday, never giving it a thought. We either wore them thin or out grew them.

We walked to The Hightower Baptist Church, which had been a school when my Mother was growing up. The neighbors who lived above us walked also, The Fred Ammons Family. Below us lived the Vance Winchester family who also walked . We kids went without an adult many times because my Mother was sick with a heart condition, and was unable to walk there and back. We would either walk with the Winchester Family or the Ammons Family. My Daddy did not attend regularly at the time. My two brothers, Marvin and Charles and my self attended regularly. We knew to "behave our selves" or we would get a peach tree limb to our backs if my Uncle Adam told our parents that we were mean. My Uncle's family had farther to walk than we did. Often their Family would go to our house for Sunday Dinner and stay all evening until it was Church time again. Mama and Grandma would always have a big dinner cooked by the time we returned from Church. Chicken and dumplings were served frequently, as we grew our own chickens for the egg supply and for the meat. There would always be a very large pot of potatoes and vegetables from the garden either fresh or home canned from the root cellar. Hot biscuits with home made butter and lots of fresh cows milk to drink. Jams and jellies were available.

To make chicken and dumplings you will need: A big fat dressed hen boiled in a large pot of water until tender. Remove the bones from the chicken. Salt and pepper to taste. Mama always made the biscuits as she made the dumplings. She used self-rising flour and enough heavy cream to make soft dough. This was rolled out thin with the dough roller. A tin biscuit cutter was used to cut the biscuits from the dough. The scraps were re-rolled until thin, and cut into long strips. The chicken would be boiling; each strip of dough was broken into small pieces and dropped into the boiling broth. A lid was placed on the pot and it was moved to the backside of the stove to simmer for 15 minutes without removing the lid. After the time passed the lid was removed and the dumplings gently stirred. The biscuits would bake in about the same amount of time.

The thing about cooking back then, you cooked a very large pot of several things. If anything wasn't ate by the end of the day it was fed to the hogs or chickens. There usually wasn't much left over with eight people to feed if no company was present. There was always bread in the cupboard. If all of the bread was eaten, another pan would be baked so if any one came during the night that was hungry there would be some bread and milk to feed them.

There wasn't room around the table for everyone. The adults ate at the table; we kids either waited until they were finished or ate somewhere else. By the time we finished dinner and did the dishes it would be three o'clock. The grown-up's sat on the porch and talked while us kids played softball or dodge the cow patty. (This was actually a game of throwing dry cow patties at each other.) It sounds gross now but then it was "just a game".

Adam's wife was named Elvira we just called her Aunt Vary. They had eleven children. Their names are Tiney, Arnold, Maylee, Mildred, Maxine, R.L.. Barbara, Marie, Shirley, Bobby and Becky, or these are the names they went by then. Some are nick names. Some of the older ones were married. The ones who came home with us were R.L who was a little older than my brother Marvin. Barbara who was Marvin's age, Marie who was a little younger than me. Shirley who was my brother Charles's age or close. Later Bobby and Becky came along. Sometimes more young people of the neighbor hood would come to our house to play. Before we knew it, we would need to get cleaned up and ready to go back to the evening service, which started at seven o'clock on Sunday night and also on Wednesday night.

The services were well attended back then, "saved or sinner". The "sinners" usually remained out side the church house. Church was the only community social to attend. The "biggest sin" was the consumption of alcohol. Homemade Moonshine. Making whisky back then was considered a "trade". Good whisky makers were well known and respected by some, or perhaps many. Almost every family kept a little whisky on hand and used it as medicine. Whisky with some bitter herbs mixed into it, would "cure" just about anything from colds and sore throats to stomach cramps. I am not sure the "cure" came so much from the whisky, but possibly the concoction tasted so awful we did not dare complain of any ailments, If it wasn't mixed with herbs, the cure possibly came from the amount consumed, if consuming continued one would be taken into a drunken stupor. I want to tell you of the bad effects of whisky, because that was the Churches biggest rival.

The serious risk of drinking alcohol, other than in small amounts as a medicine, is the forming of a craving, which permits the bounds of moderation to be over-passed. Thus allowing the demon of addiction to rule ones life. Those very demons held some of the men in our community captive. My Daddy not excluded. Occasionally the Preacher would be so full of the Holy Ghost of God that strong holds of the demons could be broken by His preaching and praying combined with the praying efforts of the God fearing Deacons and members of the Church. All credit going to God. I knew three of these preachers. Reverend Tom Pilky, we called him Preacher Tom. Reverend Martin Cable, called Preacher Cable and Reverend Ed Cook, called Preacher Cook.

Sometimes the "new man" was able to stay "right" and other times He would be attacked by the demons at a vulnerable moment and "off the wagon He fell" much to the agony of his family and Church friends. Finally my Daddy was delivered from the demons and continued on in the faith until death.

All around, the neighborhood was a safe place to live and rear children. The less said, to a person overcome by too much alcohol, the better. The evils of today are many and remain rivals of the Church. The Hightower Baptist Church is still in the same spot as then. The Church has had several face-lifts. The same spirit of God prevails there now as then. A few of the same people are attending there yet. My Mother probably the oldest regular member attending now.

By the time we would get home from Church at night, It would be away past our bed time, We would drift off to sleep thinking about the next rest day. The Sabbath.

OUR LINK TO THE OUTSIDE WORLD

Marvin joined the 4-H club and chose a pig as his project. The project worked like this: a pig was furnished to a boy or girl. They feed and cared for the pig until she was full-grown. The sow pig was then bred to a male hog. Baby pigs arrived later. When those baby pigs were six weeks old one pig was given back to the 4-H club to be given to another child. The other pigs were to be sold and the profit was Marvin's after the feed bill and any other bills were paid. Pigs were selling for ten dollars each.

Marvin got his six-week-old pig and named her Susie. Susie was a pretty little pink pig. She became sort of a family pet instead of a farm animal. The whole family took an interest in Susie. Marvin and Daddy made a pig lot for her to roam in. A pigpen was in the lot.

Susie received a lot of attention; she began to follow Marvin around like a puppy dog does. Soon she was growing so fast. Marvin was faithful to feed Susie. After school the first thing Marvin did was to go to the lot and play with the pig and feed her.

Susie loved to roll in the mud; she would be covered from head to tail in mud. I guess all pigs love mud. Finally Susie was a grown up sow. It was discovered that Susie was ready for a boy friend. Cecil Dorsey came to our house with his big Yorkshire boar hog, He was unloaded into the pen with Susie. Susie was given some "privacy" we were shooed off to play. I enjoyed playing with the Dorsey girls, Vicky and Donna. They were so cute and little.

Susie started eating even more with each meal. Soon she was putting on weight. Susie was going to be a mother. One hundred and twelve days from the visit with her boy friend, Susie gave birth to twelve plump little pink piglets. Ten of the pigs were healthy happy pigs. All looked exactly like their mother, and father too for that matter. I don't know who was the proudest, Susie, Marvin or Mama. Little pink piglets were running all around the place in no time. Each one seemed to get bigger each and every day. At the age of six weeks one pig would go to another boy or girl in the 4-H Club.

Marvin let the leader of the club know when the pig would be ready to wean from the mother. Finally the day came when one little piglet would have to leave home and go to a new place. The pick of the litter was soon on her way. That left Marvin with nine little pink piglets. Word of mouth advertising soon brought other interested people to our door looking to buy a pig. Pigs sold for ten dollars each. Marvin kept a pig to raise and fatten. All the others sold.

After all the bills were paid Marvin had made a profit. He bought a radio with the money. Up to this time we had no contact with the outside world at all, except through word of mouth and news repeated at school. No radio or television.

A radio was so fascinating. Now we could hear music any time we wanted. On Friday nights we could listen to the country music shows by radio. We heard of "I Like Ike" and the song Yellow Purple People Eater or Walla Walla Bing Bang. Any way we thought we were right up town with the new radio. Marvin was as proud of that radio as he had been the new pig and the new mama with lots of little pigs.

We were all indebted to Marvin for our link to the outside world. The radio played music at a certain time each morning. That was the fist alarm clock in the house. Up till now Daddy woke up every morning at about the same time with the help of the old red rooster.

My Grandma thought the radio was an abomination to God. She did not like for the radio to play much. If we were making any kind of body movement with the music we were quickly reprimanded by Grandma. There would be no dancing in this house.

We heard the first presidential speeches that year. Not the first but the first to us. We also heard preaching and singing on the radio.

That was okay with Grandma. The radio belonged to Marvin but it was enjoyed by the whole family.

EIGHTH GRADE

In 1962 I was in the eighth grade at Almond Elementary School in the Lauada Community which was located about five miles west of Bryson City, N. C. I had gone to the same school since beginning the first grade.

Mr. Cowan Wikle was my eighth grade teacher as well as the school principal. Mr. Wikle was a very compassionate man; he also was a very serious man when it came to schoolwork. Mr. Wikle expected each one to do the very best they could. When he discovered a special talent within a student, he encouraged you to develop that talent to the fullest. I was good in math and Mr. Wikle challenged me with more and more advanced math problems, as he did a few other students in the class. He was a wonderful teacher.

We were still very poor; Mama was still battling heart problems. My Daddy did not have a steady job; just what he could pick up here and there and sold some pulpwood and logs. We did not have money to buy our lunch, which was only 20 cents at that time. There were five kids in school then. We carried our lunch to school in a brown paper bag and saved the wax paper and bag to carry lunch in the next day.

I had never eaten in the lunchroom at school except the few times at Christmas when every one got to eat. I imagine the teachers were the ones who made sure each child ate the special dinner cooked for the holiday. Mr. Wikle made an announcement that he needed someone to clean the erasers and wash the blackboard each day in return for lunch. There were two of us girls who wanted to do that. I remember her name but do not wish to embarrass her by mentioning her name. Mr. Wikle decided to allow both of us to do the chore, alternating week about. Every other week I ate in the lunchroom and stayed in for about fifteen minutes of the recess period and worked for my lunch. The next week she did the same. We each carried our lunch the other week.

Mr. Wikle's wife, Mrs. Edna Wikle was a wonderful woman. She was a stay at home mom, with one daughter named Sandra who was a few years ahead of me in school. Mrs. Wikle had been involved with the school for all the years I had been going there. She volunteered when needed, substituted for teachers when they needed to be off or were sick. Mrs. Wikle was a frisky little woman; her size was enhanced by her determination and expectations. She did not put up with any foolishness. Mrs. Wikle, like her husband had the kindest heart. She and some other ladies of the community ran a clothing room at the school. Mrs. Bertha Dehart and Mrs. Beasley were regulars in the clothing room too. They kept me in clothes, other than the hand-me-downs from cousin Emma and the feed sack dresses which was one a year. The clothing room kept my whole family in clothes.

As the school year progressed into early spring we became excited over the soon to be graduation. The girls were to wear white dresses and the boys navy slacks and white shirts. The girls were talking about their new dresses and pumps. I knew I had no way of getting new clothing. Mrs. Wikle came to school every Wednesday to work in the clothing room. One day she came to our classroom and asked me to see her at recess. I went to where she was working in the clothing room. Mrs. Wikle asked me if I needed a new dress for graduation. I told her that I did not have one. Mrs. Wikle took out her measuring tape and began to measure me. She wrote down several different measurements. She also asked me what size shoes I wore.

The next week Mrs. Wikle asked me to come to the clothing room again. I went. She had made me a beautiful white dress with a baby blue cummerbund belt (a wide gathered belt that snapped together, fashionable at that time.) Blue and white was our school colors. There was a new pair of white pumps; I had never had pumps before. (Dressy shoes with a little heel). There was brand-new underclothing in my size. I would not believe my eyes. Mrs. Wikle had me take the things to the bus so other kids did not see them. Kids can be cruel at times, I knew I was poor I did not need comments made and that often happened.

Mrs. Wikle knew that we did not have a vehicle and would need a ride to the school for graduation. She volunteered to come to my house and pick my family and me up and take us there and back home. What a lady! My Mama would not allow her to do this for our family, even though we were very thankful for the offer.

Mr. Glen Breedlove was the driver of our school bus at that time. Glen had a truck bigger than a regular pickup with slats extending the bed of the truck up to the cab. Mama told me to ask Glen if he would take us to the graduation. He said he would take us there and stay for the graduation and bring us home again for three dollars. He was not planning on going otherwise. We got together the three dollars to pay him. Our whole family could get on the back of the truck; it was no big thing to ride the back. We were glad to get any ride. The women rode up front and the rest rode the back. I stayed at the Beasley home after school so I did not have to ride the back of the truck to the school. I graduated from the eighth grade wearing new clothes.

Glen Breedlove was a very nice man and very funny, he was always playing a prank on someone and laughing about it. He was also an asset to our community. He was "accommodating" meaning willing to help others. When there were not many cars, people hauled other people to town for supplies and etc. for a fee. That was a way of making a little extra money for them. It was a lot cheaper than hiring a taxi.

Glen loved the bread called sweetbread, mentioned before. I guess about every one was familiar with the bread. Somehow Glen ended up with the nickname "Sweetbread".

A lot of people called him by that name. I don't remember how it was started. I am printing the recipe below in memory of Mr. Glen Breedlove.

Sweetbread

Mix one cup of molasses or honey with one egg, two cups of flour and enough milk to make a batter. Pour into a greased baking pan and bake until golden brown. Remove and cool, cut into slices.

HIGH SCHOOL

In the fall of 1962 I entered the ninth grade at Swain County High School. My older brother Marvin was entering the eleventh grade and so was my cousin Emma. They both helped me find my way around.

Emma took me under her wing and allowed me to tag along with her and her friends. I never tried to really make friends of my own. I was a very shy person. Some of my former classmates were also in some of my classes in ninth grade.

My family was still almost as poor as before, except my Mama did not require the expensive medication as at one time. My Mama was doing a lot better but still not able to work on a public job. My Daddy still picked up odd jobs and continued to work in the woods cutting logs along as he could. The tobacco crop was in the field, no money from that until the middle of December.

My Mama had managed to save a few dollars and took me to town to buy a new dress for school The store was having a sale on dresses, buy one and get one free. I had never been shopping before. I had never gotten a store bought dress in my life until now. I was so excited. I bought a pretty brown print dress and got a gray/black plaid free. I had one other dress that I could wear that was given to me. I started ninth grade with three dresses. This meant I had to wear two of the dresses twice each week.

We usually got two pencils at the beginning of school and no more until the tobacco check came. In high school notebooks were needed for each class. I did get those and one pack of notebook paper. My one pack of twenty-five sheets of paper did not last very long. I was soon out of paper with no money to buy any more.

I was sitting in the front row in this one class. No one I knew was sitting near me. I learned the names of two girls sitting close to me. One was Terry and the other one was Sherry Jacks. I asked to borrow a sheet of paper from one of them every day. Sherry asked me why I didn't have any paper; I just said, "I don't have any money to buy paper". Every time we needed paper, Sherry just gave me a sheet of paper. She never one time asked me when I could repay her. When the tobacco check came I did get more paper. I tried to repay Sherry; she would not take the paper back. I have never forgotten her kindness

Thank you, Sherry.

That summer my Mama got a job cooking at the Tote and Tarry Restaurant in the Nantahala Gorge, which later became the Nantahala Outdoor Center. I had gotten a job at the Smoky Mountain Restaurant in Bryson City working with Ruth Ammons and Barbara Sutton. After Mama got the job at the restaurant, she got me a waitress job with her. I left my first job after a month and worked with my Mama. I managed to save enough money to buy my school clothes. I got five outfits, one for each day. I bought school supplies for the whole year and had money to eat in the cafeteria at school. I did not have to borrow paper anymore.

My Daddy got a regular job that year with Colville Construction Company. That was a turn around for our family. We never got rich but we were able to buy what was needed for the family.

I still worked during the summers while in High School. I went to work at Nantahala Village as a waitress and worked there for eight summers. The good thing about waiting tables was the tips. Every day I got paid in tips.

My Mama worked at several different places. She worked in the school cafeteria . She got a job at Nantahala Village and worked there for over thirty years.

THE WAY THINGS WERE

Emma is my double first cousin, our mothers are sisters and our fathers were brothers. There were two years different in the ages of our mothers and the same with our fathers. They were very close as family.

As long as I can remember Emma was just always there as was my brother Marvin. Emma was an only child and she had a lot more toys and things than we did. Emma had pretty hair bows for her hair, I did not have any. She always shared with me.

When I was four years old I started staying all night at Emma's house. We did not always see eye to eye. As long as I did to suit Emma things were fire. Often I did my own thing, and a quarrel was underway. We quarreled quiet a bit and always departed as friends.

As we grew up most people thought we were sisters and we were as close as sisters. I got her hand-me-downs, thank goodness. Aunt

Edna made a lot of Emma's clothes. One time she made us all matching red plaid wool skirts. That was my all time favorite skirt. We wore them at the same time, Aunt Edna, Emma and I.

I always enjoyed staying at their house at night. If Aunt Edna wasn't selling milk, she was selling eggs. I loved to sort and clean the eggs. It had to be just right or Aunt Edna would make me redo it. Uncle Lloyd loved to tell funny stories. He and Daddy grew up in a very large family. There were lots of funny things to tell.

Uncle Lloyd was afraid of honeybees. He would get sick if he was stung by the bees. (this may be where I got the bee alergy). Grandpa Sutton raised bees for the honey. Honey sold for three or four dollars by the gallon . Any dollar made was a dollar to help out. Uncle Lloyd hated the bees; He threatened to put sulfur powder in the bee gums. Grandpa Sutton got word of it. Grandpa told Lloyd that he had better not bother the bees or he would have to contend with Grandpa. No one wanted to go against Grandpa. Uncle Lloyd walked around the bees and did not harm them in any way. Grandpa demanded respect from his grown up children and he got respect too.

The bees were funny creatures. There was only one queen bee in a hive or gum. The bees killed all other queen bees. If one other queen bee survived and started to boss the hive, the old queen left the hive and all the other bees went with her except for just a few. The old queen would find a hollow log or old bee gum and set up in it. The lighter honey is made from sourwood blossoms or corn tassels. Clover is a favorite also. The Sourwood tree blooms about the same time the early corn tassels. Honey is sometimes called Sourwood honey and may be corn tassel honey. If you have worked in a vegetable garden, you have probably seen the bees "working the corn tassels" To help locate a bee tree in the woods a little flour was dusted onto the bees. The bees were timed to see how long it took the bees to travel to thier home. The direction the bee flew was closely monitored. It might take a while but eventually the tree was found.

Uncle Lloyd always teased me. My nickname was Bunt. He would call me Blunt. Uncle Lloyd was also scared of snakes especially poison ones. He did not want any thing to do with them. Uncle Lloyd liked to "nip the bottle", meaning he liked to drink whisky. The more he drank the funnier he was unless of course he went beyond the bounds of moderation. If that happened Uncle would "sleep it off".

My Aunt Edna was a very independent woman, fairly large in stature and strong in will and body. Aunt Edna worked like a man at any task before her. We kids never feared any thing as long as she was with us. Well not unless we became the target for her outlet of anger with rightful cause. I knew I would not be spared the rod if I indeed did need it. Aunt Edna took care of the discipline to all children when it was needed. She did not prolong the misery. I love my Aunt

Edna and have always held a high respect for her. I think I inherited a few traits from her for myself.

Aunt Edna made the prettiest things out of the most ordinary items. Today that is called "arts and crafts". Back then to her it was just a way of life. Aunt Edna could turn a scrap of cloth into a beautiful pull string purse in just a few minutes on the old Singer petal sewing machine. She has continued to create beautiful things all my life. She could make a beautiful cake for any occasion. I did acquire that gift with a lot of help from the Lord. I also love making things.

Emma had fingernail polish. I begged for her to paint my nails. She always did. I had no polish of my own until I was in the eighth grade. Isabel Willis got my name at Christmas and bought me a bottle of beautiful pink nail polish and put a pretty ribbon on the gift. I will never forget that gift.

One day we were cooking supper. Aunt Edna made the best green peas that I have ever eaten. She grew them in the garden. The peas were shelled and cooked in a pan with some water. Cream and a little flour were added to the end of the cooking to make creamed peas. Aunt Edna told me to stir the peas. I started to stir the peas and I stirred some onto the top of the wood cook stove. They sizzled and smoked. Emma said, "Do you not know how to stir peas? Let me show you." Emma started to stir the peas and she did the same as I did, some came out of the pan and ran onto the stove sizzling and smoking same as mine. I started laughing and couldn't quit laughing. The more I laughed the madder Emma got and the more peas she stirred onto the stove. Aunt Edna took over and shooed us both out of the kitchen. We had to carry in the wood and carry water for the night. I laughed the whole way. Finally Emma got over the embarrassment and started laughing too. The next time we had to stir the peas we were very careful not to stir them onto the stove.

Emma was playing at our house one day; Aunt Edna had gone to town. Emma cut her hand. Mama got really scared and did not know what to do. She poured salt into the cut. Emma had a little lump in the wound even after it healed. She would tell people "that is where Aunt Pauline poured salt into my cut".

We went barefoot everywhere. Often times we cut our feet on glass or rocks. The worst thing was a stumped toe or (stubbed toe). We called it stumped toe. The big toe was usually the one affected. That thing would swell up and be so sore. Grandma would use homemade salve from the Balm of Gillead tree. She would put the salve on a white rag and wrap the toe, then she would bring a piece of the rag around our ankle and tie it in a knot. What a sight! Usually before the toe healed we would bump it again several times. That salve smelled awful. The white bandage did not stay clean for long. Going with out shoes, the bandage became a dirty mess. I have recently expermented in the making of that salve. She used the salve for about all skin wounds.

During Dog Days no sore would heal properly. If you had a cut or sore of any kind on the feet and got out early in the morning in the dew the sore wouldn't heal. It was called "dew poisoning". Blood poisoning was a possibility. Blood poisoning was very dangerous and required a lot of soaking in hot water with Epson salts applied. A sulfur powder poultice (which was the home-made salve and sulfur powder mixed) would be applied to the affected area. If that didn't bring the poisoning out, a trip to the doctor was unavoidable. We avoided Doctor visits if at all possible. My brother Charles got blood posing one time and did not tell any one until it was really bad. He ended up in the hospital for several days.

If we caught a cold during the winter, Grandma would rub groundhog grease on our throat and chest. That stuff was awful. I was glad to have the Vicks vapor rub instead of the groundhog grease. I never got an earache or "strepthroat" during my childhood. (That is a different story now)

There was a peddler who came around to the houses back then, selling any and everything imaginable. At least He could order it if the item wasn't readily available.

There was a "taking lineament" for the ales of the stomach. The usual dose was a spoonful in a cup of warm water. The stuff was strong. We had also bought some real cough syrup that tasted really good. I was coughing one night continuously. My Daddy got out of bed and was going to give me a dose of cough syrup. The bottles were very much alike. Daddy got the lineament and poured out a spoonful and gave it to me. I swallowed it right down thinking I was swallowing the cough medicine. The lineament was so strong that it took my breath away. It scared my Daddy and me. I did not cough any more that night. I was afraid to cough. I did not want any more medicine. Later we decided the lineament was better cough medicine than the regular cough syrup was

My Cousin Emma

If ever I was in a dilemma
The person I called was Emma.
You have been in my life from the start.
Everything I did you were a part.
Our houses were so close together
We could play in any type of weather.
You had a lot of toys and dolls with hair.
I loved to play with your things, you would share.
You were an only child until much later.
I was one of five, the need was greater.
For sewing your Mom had a knack.
Dresses were beautiful made from feedsack.
I was glad for you to hand them down to me.
Sometimes the hem came below my knee.
You had make-up, nail polish, powder and cologne.
I sampled everything; you said, "How much did you put on?"
You got drivers license and a car.
We could travel near and far.
In order to be with thee
Your friends had to tolerate me.
The years have come and gone
My love for you remains strong. I love you, Emma

My Mama had one set of dishes when she and my Daddy were married. Mama had sold stuff and got the dishes. They were beautiful milk glass with gold trim around the top. Mama tried to save the dishes for special occasions. Five kids can be very detrimental to glass dishes. We tried to be careful but sometimes it just happened, one would get broken Companies knew people would not buy plates, cups, saucers and other things when the family needed flour, sugar and oatmeal. The companies started putting dishes in the sacks or boxes of essentials. A dinner plate came in a sack of flour. Depending on how often flour was needed, one might collect a set of plates before the company put a different item in the sacks. Oatmeal usually contained a cup or saucer. That is how we got our dishes. The flour came in pillowcases at one time. (25 lb.) We always used the big sacks of flour. A metal measuring cup was an item we got out of the grocery bags. We had metal drinking cups that came in a box of something. We also had snuff glasses since Grandma used snuff. Each snuff glass held eight ounces, the exact amount in one cup.

I still have a few of those glasses. I pick one up at the yard sale occasionally "just to be doing" that was a favorite saying when there was no real reason for doing something.

We always had enough food while growing up. Occasionally we would run out of flour and have to eat cornbread for breakfast. Mama would fry some potatoes and make eggs and gravy to go with the corn bread. I love honey on hot cornbread for breakfast or any time.

One time I remember our potatoes were "running out" meaning we did not have enough potatoes to last until new potatoes came in. After peeling the potatoes to cook Mama saved the potato peelings to plant. Potatoes grew from those peelings.

A favorite food using cornbread for breakfast was scrambled eggs and cornbread mixed together like an omelet. It is very good. Grandma loved this and did not limit it to when there was no flour. She would use left over corn bread.

There were times when "times" were really hard. I remember carrying my milk to school in a very small mayonnaise jar because we did not have three cents to buy milk. I always carried biscuits to school and most of the kids who carried their lunch carried loaf bread. I remember swapping lunches with Deloris Phillips. She had loaf bread with potted meat. I had biscuits with eggs.

One day the dog ate my lunch; this was while we had to walk down the road to catch the school bus. Violet Winchester fixed me another lunch; it was her dog that ate my lunch.

One morning I had been waiting for the bus inside Violets house, when we heard the bus coming up the road we ran to the bus house and got our books. This particular day I jumped off the porch as usual and it had rained. I slipped in the mud and was covered. Violet gave me one of Cathy's dresses to wear to school. It was a really pretty navy floral with a white color. It was a store bought dress. That was the first store bought dress I had ever worn. Violet helped me get washed up while the bus waited for me. Violet's Dad drove the bus at that time.

THE GIFT

The whole family petted my two younger sisters. Linda was petted most by my Daddy who took care of her more than the others because my Mama was sick while she was small. Dianne was petted because she was so sick and almost died when in the hospital at twenty-two months of age with the pneumonia. She was also the baby of the family and the older kids petted her.

The "little girls" were spared from doing chores at an early age. I thought they should help with the dishes and have responsibilities the same as I had, at their age. There were times when we strongly disagreed on things. They usually won.

The little girls did have some restrictions that we older children did not have; they could not go outside and play in the cold weather like we could. I enjoyed the wintertime and still do today. Snow was my favorite kind of weather.

As the years went by we were all growing up, first my older brother left home to go to college, My younger brother left home and then I was getting married. My little sisters were growing up too. There was still a shortage of money, but not like earlier years. My Daddy had a regular job at this time. My sisters did not have any means of making money, yet they saved every extra penny that they could to buy me a wedding gift.

There was a shower held for me. My little sisters proudly gave me the gift that they had saved for, shopped for, and wrapped up for me. I knew they had made a sacrifice for me. I was hesitant to open the gift, I felt bad they had spent their money on a gift for me. Their faces held eager smiles as I opened the gift.

As years have come and gone, I remember vaguely some of the things that were given to me at the shower. The one gift I will never forget is the beautiful set of salt and pepper shakers that my little sisters gave to me.

A true gift of love.

FAMILY AT CHRISTMAS TIME

Christmas has always been my favorite holiday. I love to see the frost so thick it looks like a light snow. The only weather better is snow, of course.

December was the most exciting month of the year. The tobacco crop check usually came around the fifteenth of the month. School let out about the twentieth for the holidays. We started combing the mountains for the perfect or near perfect Christmas tree. Christmas Eve and Christmas Day were very exciting times.

Mama usually bought us kids one new thing for Christmas. We were not taught there was a Santa Claus. We knew better, because there were no presents under the tree on Christmas morning. Mama gave us what she bought the same day she bought it. The one item usually was a pair of jeans or shoes, whichever was needed most. When I was in the fifth grade I begged my Mama for a purse. All the other girls were carrying a purse to school. That year I got a pretty red bucket-like purse with a fold over top, the very most popular purse at that time. I was thrilled to death with the new purse. I carried that purse for three years, much longer than the purse was in style.

As soon as school let out, my Brothers and I would head off to the woods looking for that perfect tree. We were very familiar with the hills surrounding our house. We had been over every foot of the property. We cut a cedar, white pine or sometimes a yellow pine. One time we cut a holly bush. That was a big mistake and was not repeated. The holly pricked our fingers when we placed the decorations on the limbs. We had a few special ornaments used year after year, but mostly our decorations were hand made by us kids. We strung popcorn with a needle and thread to make a rope to drape around the tree. We also made paper ropes at school. We did not have any electric lights, yet we thought the tree was beautiful.

We were involved in the annual Christmas play at Hightower Baptist Church. There was always the Holy family nativity scene consisting of Mary, Joseph and of course the baby Jesus. There were angels singing praises to the new born King. The church was usually full on Christmas Eve. The most attended service of the year. Christmas carols were sung by the congregation as well as specials during the play. There were wrapped up gifts for every one who drew names. The gift was often a box of cherry candy or stick peppermint candy, sometimes a toy or game or coloring book with crayons. The gifts were kept under the Christmas tree until after the play ended. The gifts were then handed out to their rightful owners. A sack of candy, nuts, apples, oranges, gum and a big candy bar inside was given to each child and to all adults if there were enough to go around. We would have a lot of the candy ate by the time we walked back home.

We were pretty excited, you see we seldom got candy during the year; it was a real treat to get just one piece of candy. Mama sometimes would buy a roll of thin wafer candy about the size of a nickel. There were lots of different colors in the roll. We five kids would share the roll, giving each of us five or six thin nickel size wafers of candy. That candy is still available today. I buy one occasionally just because of the memories.

My Mama and Grandma started baking goodies several days before Christmas. We would have a half dozen different kinds of cakes and pies. There was always the old time stack apple cake. Coconut was a favorite, as was black walnut cake with the walnuts inside the cake and in the icing, also chocolate cake. There were also chocolate pie, lemon pie pumpkin pie, sweet potato pie, gingerbread black walnut pie and others. The list got longer as the years went on, trying to get everyone's favorite included. I read about there being thirteen desserts for Christmas. One for Jesus and each of the disciples. I think that must have been the reason for so many kinds of dessert at our house. The other reason could have been the tobacco check came just in time to stock up on supplies for the season's baking needs.

On Christmas morning we were up bright and early. Mama would set out the mixed nuts, which consisted of English walnuts, Brazil nuts, Hazel nuts, almonds, and pecans. She usually saved the black walnuts to bake and make fudge with. After breakfast we would start cracking those nuts. We would set a cast iron pressing iron in our lap and use it for a base to crack the nuts. We had a couple of hammers and three or four of the irons. We had to take turns, causing quiet a ruckus. We played with any new toys or colored in the coloring books until it would be noon.

Our Uncle Everett always came to Christmas dinner. My aunt Edna, Uncle Lloyd and Emma came sometimes. My Grandma's other children would usually come for a short visit sometime during the day. There were eight of us so we always had a crowd at the table. The table was about eight foot long and three feet wide. It would accommodate a crowd.

If the weather was fair, not raining or snowing the men folk would go rabbit hunting. I would get to tag along sometimes. If there was snow on the ground all the kids, except the two little sisters, would go snow sled riding in the pasture. We just had home- made sleds, but they sure were enjoyed. A couple hours later we would go back to the warm fire to thaw out our feet and hands.

We would not have a cooked meal at night. There was always lots of left over food and goodies. With all the extra sugar consumed during the day we were not sleepy at bedtime. We were allowed to sit up and play a board game called Wahoo. This was a game similar to the modern SORRY game of today. My Daddy and Mama made the board. The game was taught to us by Alvin and Maude Breedlove (as mentioned before.) We have enjoyed playing that game ever since. The homemade board was a lot more fun than the store bought version.

The first year that I had a wrapped up gift under our Christmas tree on Christmas morning was the year my brother Marvin got married to a girl named Pat Marlow. I was in the eleventh grade. My gift was a really nice perfume set from Avon. I will never forget that gift. Every one in our family had a wrapped up gift. That was when the family tradition was started. Thank you Marvin. My parents both were not used to gifts being wrapped and under the Christmas tree.

Over the years our family grew, with different ones getting married. I married Roy Parton in 1967. My Grandma died in July of 1971. Her death left a big hole in our family. She has been greatly missed. My brother Charles married Linda Cox in 1972. In 1973 Timmy was born to them just a few days before I gave birth to Kevin. The first grandchildren. Dianne married Melvin Jones and Paula was born later that same year. Three grandchildren in less than a year. The next year Lyle was born to Marvin and Margaret Davis (this was

Marvin's second marriage). In 1975 Christopher Parton was born just a few days before Misty Jones, in early 1976 Christy Sutton was born to Charles and Linda. This made a total of seven grandchildren born in less than three years. Linda remained childless.

There was no longer room for the whole family to get around the kitchen table all at the same time. The little children would eat around the coffee table.

Our family continued to be together as much as possible at Christmas time. There were times when some had to work, others lived away. The family changed due to marriage, divorce, death and birth, Marvin's wife and Lyle's mother, Margaret died at age 39 with breast cancer. Our hearts were greatly saddened by her death. Divorces and death left hearts broken and children suffering. Life must go on for all the living. Time is a healer. Children learn to cope with situations beyond their control usually better than adults do.

Jennifer Ingle joined our family; she and Charles were married in 1986. A month later I suddenly found myself a single woman and not by choice. Daniel was born in 1989. The grandchildren totaled 8. God replaced the void in my life with a wonderful man. Raymond Cochran is my soul mate if there is such a thing. Raymond has one son named Bart. Bart and I clashed from the beginning. Raymond is a very patient man. I was very strict with my children, yet I loved them more than life. The day Kevin graduated from high school, Chris got his drivers license. I cried all day. As time went on and

I look back that day was not so bad, there were worse ones on the way. The loneliest day was the day after Kevin got married and left home. Chris was already married. Grandchildren bring laughter, renewed love and an opportunity to view the world through the eyes of a child again. They are precious.

Paula made my parents great grandparents with her daughter Cynthia Shields. Dianne and Melvin Jones are now the first grandparents in the family. I follow the next year with grandson David Troy Parton, parents Christopher Parton and Angela McMahan Parton.

Our hearts were saddened again with the death of Tim's infant son Shawn Sutton.

Marvin had another son born in 1989 named Patrick Bryson. Marvin is a grandpa to Sharlot and Austin Sutton. Born to Lyle and Donna Sutton. David has already been mentioned, a wonderful grandson now age twelve. Then there was his baby sister Mellanie who was born three months premature who will soon be six years old. Mellanie has had a struggle walking, she has to wear braces. We think Mellanie is a miracle child! Mellanie weighted in at two pounds and six ounces at birth. She dropped down to one pound and ten ounces before she started gaining weight. Mayson Faith was born a year later to Kevin and Mary Dills Parton. She is a delight. Being a grandparent is a wonderful thing

Bart and April Messick Cochran have two beautiful children that like me a lot better than Bart ever did. Raymond is a wonderful grandpa to all five grandchildren. I am teaching Dylan and Alyssa Cochran to call me "Gramma" they are my grandchildren too. Dylan loves his "Paw Paw".

Charles has one grandson named Cody. Cody is a "fireball", and a delightful child. Being a grandpa and the father of a teenager is probably what keeps Charles acting younger than his age. Jennifer says it is because she is raising Daniel while Charles is off working, and Charles gets to "play" when he is home. Cody is Tim's son. Daniel is a carbon copy of his dad. Christy is married to Sam Brown and they have no children.

Dianne and Melvin are the only ones to celebrate a silver wedding anniversary. Congratulations! They are grandparents to five children. Cynthia mentioned before has a brother named Joshua Shields, son of Paula and Matthew Shields. Anna, Tyasia and Dabrena Postel daughters of Misty and Mark Postel.

Linda has no children of her own, but has always liked children and bestowed motherly-like love on many children. Linda has changed her last name a few times.

There are about 35 people to get together at Christmas time. Last year we did not have a big get together. My Daddy was sick and just home from the hospital. He was not physically able for a big crowd. Christmas was not the usual. It was my Daddy's last Christmas. He went home to be with the Lord on February the eighth, 2004. The loss is so great. I miss him so very much,. My mother has lost her mate of nearly 58 years. It is tough on her. The living must go on living until their appointed time of departure from this earth. Linda is living in the house with Mama and they are good for each other.

Our family will never be the same again. We have to accept new roles in life. I will never be my daddy's little girl again. As long as my Daddy was alive I knew I was still just his little girl. Now I am a wife, mother and grandmother. I must continue to fill those roles. Christmas will be different this year, but it will still be Christmas, the reason to celebrate has not changed.

We celebrate the birth of our Lord and Savior Jesus Christ. If you do not know Jesus as your Lord and Savior, I invite you right now to ask Him to forgive you of your sins and come into your heart to live. I hope you will do this, and you will have a real reason to celebrate Christmas this year. I hope all of my family have accepted Jesus as their personal Savior and will celebrate with me the true meaning of Christmas.

This book did not get finished as I had planned. Christmas came with bitter sweetness. The whole family was together except Charles's daughter Christy. We all missed Daddy so much. Mama's friend and Raymond's mother Faye Cochran joined our family for lunch. Faye lost her only daughter Wanda in early December. We were glad to have her with us. She was a brave woman to join the big crowd.

MAKING A QUILT

Any one can make a quilt if you can sew at all. My Grandmother showed me how to make quilts when I was a little girl. There are hundreds of quilt patterns out there. This particular quilt does not need a special pattern. You can make your own pattern. This was one of my Grandma's favorites.

You will need a lot of scraps of cloth, or you can buy some material at the cloth shop. My Grandma never bought a scrap of cloth for quilt making. She salvaged cloth from all possible sources. Any scraps left over from making clothing from the feed sacks, any scraps the neighbors gave to her and the ones saved from the sides of clothing. The sides took less wear and tear than the front or back of the garments.

This quilt is constructed of what is called a "square". Each square was made up of nine smaller squares. You can use any color arrangement that you like. I like to have a solid color to "set" the quilt together, and a different solid color coordinating with a print or flowered fabric.

Cut a square piece of paper any size you want 4", 5", or 6". You now have the only pattern piece needed for this quilt. Say you choose 6". You will need five 6" squares alike. You will need four coordinating 6" squares. The combination can be your choice. Sew one solid square to one floral and add another solid. You now have one row of three 6" squares. You will need three rows to make what is called a "quilt square". Make another row the same as the first one. Next sew the opposite; sew one floral then a solid then a floral. Sew the last row you just finished in between the first two rows you made. You now have nine 6" squares sewed together. This is called a "quilt square". You will need sixteen "quilt squares" to make a regular sized quilt. My grandma made what she called a "flower garden". All sixteen squares were different. You can make them all the same for a more modern look.

To "set" the quilt, MEANS TO JOIN THE QUILT SQUARES TOGETHER. You will need a six-inch piece of fabric the length of the finished quilt square; you will need one for each square and four extra. Sew a strip to one "quilt square" then add another strip. Repeat until you use four squares and five strips, a strip first and last. You should have four rows with four "quilt squares" in each row. Cut a 6" strip as long as a row of squares. You will need five of these long strips to finish "setting" the quilt. Sew a strip onto each side of a row of four squares. Continue to sew a row of squares and a strip until the "quilt top" is finished.

If you choose four or five inch squares it will take more than sixteen, Lay them out on the bed to get an idea.

In my growing up years we used a quilt frame that hung from the ceiling during quilting days and was rolled up at night. Since many people do not have access to that type of frame, I am going to tell you how to quilt with out a frame.

Select the bottom for your quilt. I usually use a sheet a size larger than I am making the quilt. Lay the sheet on the bed. Spread the quilt top on top of the sheet you will need about three or four inches more of sheet on each of the four sides. Trim accordingly. Fold the quilt top with wrong sides together, in half and in half again. You have a four-way fold. Place a big safety pin directly in the folded corner only catching two sides of fabric instead of four. Lay aside; Fold the sheet the same way. Be sure to get the "right side" out, usually the brighter side is the right side. Place a safety pin in the same place as you did in the "top". Spread the "top" back out on the bed with "right side" down. Spread the batting on top of the quilt to as close to the edges as possible. If a little hangs over, try to allow a little to hang over on all four sides. Trim if necessary. I like to buy batting on a roll and trim myself rather than buy pre cut and packaged such as the kind in department stores. If the bottom (lining) is not a pretty color that you would like to trim the top, you can cut the bottom a few inches shorter all around than the top and turn the top down instead of turning the bottom over the top, your choice.

Place the bottom on top of the batting. Be sure to line the safety pins up together by putting one hand underneath the quilt and adjusting so as to be even with the top pin. You can do this on your kitchen table also. Whether on the bed or the table, you will need to either pin the edges all around or base stitch then and later remove the thread.

I prefer to "quilt" on the table where I am more comfortable. Again fold the quilt over and have a four-way fold. Keep as straight as possible. You may fold up smaller if desired to transport to the table or to wait for another day before quilting.

When you start to quilt or tack, spread out on your table being very careful not to pucker the cloth. Start at the safety pins. To quilt means to stitch around the design or pattern, such as sew around each of the six-inch squares. To tack means to make a single large stitch at the corners only of the six-inch squares. Tacking is a lot faster, but not given the respect that true quilting receives and rightly so. It takes a long time to do true quilting. A tacked quilt will last just as long if good thread is used.

You can do tacking two ways. You can do what is called basting which is keeping the thread intact and making big stitches on all the corners. Do the entire quilt, then go back and cut between the stitches and tie a double knot with the threads and trim the thread to one half inch. The other way is to tack each corner at a time, cut and trim as you go. Always work out from the center of the quilt.

Working from the center out in all directions will help prevent puckering the quilt. It is easier to roll the quilt up to be able to reach the center better. Quilting alone is more rewarding for one self, but quilting with a friend or family member or members is a lot of fun and a good way to pass the art onto younger ones. A long time ago a girl was considered to be lazy if she did not have a half dozen hand made quilts to take to her new home after the wedding.

After quilting or tacking is completed, turn the extra fabric over or under depending on which is longer and hanging over. Turn under the raw edges and stitch either by hand or by machine. The quilt will be longer if the bottom is turned out over the top and stitched.

My Grandma pieced her quilts by hand; meaning sewed the little pieces together by hand instead of machine. Any time that my Grandma sat down, she was either knitting or piecing quilt tops. We usually had several quilt tops ready for quilting at any given time. The quilting was more time consuming and the "quilt frames" were in the way.

After we got electricity, the light was in the center of the ceiling directly over the quilt frame, when it was in its "place". The quilt blocked out the light when the quilt was rolled up at night. The frames were four pieces of smooth wooden slats a little longer than a quilt. To start quilting, a quilt was prepared as described with the batting and bottom or lining intact. the "quilt frames" had holes all the way through the wood at four or five inch intervals. There were wooden pegs or blunt nails to use in the holes. The quilt was wound around two of the slats in opposite directions. The frame and quilt resembled a table but more narrow. The side slats were secured onto the other slats with the pegs. This kept the quilt from coming unwound. The quilting started in the center, usually one or two people on each side of the quilt. The quilting process moved from the center outward. The table frame became wider with each move of the pegs and frame. This apparatus took up a big area. At times several people would trade off quilting or barter with each other. "You help me and I will help you." The girls were given a small area at the edge of the quilt to learn to get the hang of quilting. If the stitches were not even the women would "fix" the area, redo the stitching.

The churchwomen would get together and make a friendship quilt for a pastor going away present or a gift for a new bride. Each family pieced a "quilt square" and embroidered their name on the square.

Quilting is becoming more popular in recent years, but all the piecing is done on a machine. A hand made quilt used to mean just that; a quilt made entirely by hand including the sewing. Quilting methods have changed. Some sewing machines have quilting devices attached to do the actual quilting. The quilting frames are a thing of the past.

I still have a quilt that my Grandma made for me when I left home. I cherish the quilt but more appreciated is the art that she taught to me so I can make my own quilts and teach my Granddaughters to do the same if time continues. Thank you Mrs. Sarah Green for teaching me to quilt in the way described without a frame.

Another way to make a nice quilt is to sew the six inch squares of several different colors and prints of fabric, together to make the quilt as wide as you like. Sew as many rows as you want the length of the quilt to be. Use a pretty border all around to complete the quilt. There are many free quilt patterns available on the internet, as well as in books at the library.

GOOD TIMES AND FREE FUN THINGS

There are many things in life to enjoy without paying a single penny. We had to explore those possibilities when we were young as there was no money to go to amusement parks, water parks and things of that sort. We learned very early on how to be creative with nature and everyday things. Here are a few of those free things to enjoy still today.

Follow your shadow. Shadows are so much fun because they change so often depending on the time of day and the result of the sun moving across the sky. When the sun is straight above, there is no shadow. Late in the evening if you are walking toward the east with the sun going west the shadow is in front of you and is a long shadow. If you were walking west at the same time of day the shadow will be behind you. The fun possibilities are unlimited playing with your shadow. You can play with shadows from a flashlight, lamp or even the moon at night. Children love to watch their shadows. Give it a try, FREE.

There are little bugs in the ground with the entrance resembling an inverted cone. The dirt is fine and resembles sand in the "hole". These bugs come to the top of the ground with just a little persuasion. Lean close to their home and softly call, doodle bug, doodle bug and keep calling until you see the sand moving very slightly. Keep calling and the little creature will come to the top. We thought when we were kids that you had to say, "doodle bug, doodle bug come out and get some buttermilk." Well most of the children of today do not know where buttermilk comes from and the doodlebugs of today do not care to hear about the buttermilk. The little creatures will come to the top by softly calling to them.

June Bugs were great fun to play with also. The true June Bugs are big green flying bugs that resemble the green Japanese Beetles of today. Those beetles are a pest to the garden even if they do possess useful qualities in other areas. Occasionally a June bug will come by in June or maybe July They are easy to catch. With the help of another person we would tie a string onto a leg of the bug and hold the other end of the string in our hand and turn the bug loose to fly. The bug would fly around in the air above our heads depending on the length of the string. Be sure to turn the June bug loose without the string when you are finished playing with him. This may be frowned upon in today's society.

Firefly show is a very interesting thing to do in the summer at night. Watch for the little specks of light in the yard. Collect several into a glass jar with a lid. (Punch holes in the lid for air). The more people involved in the show the better. Turn out the lights and the bugs will put on the show. We called these bugs lightening bugs. Be sure to let the bugs go when finished with the show.

Cloud watching is a lot of fun too. I love to name a cloud by the shape, like dog or house, or car, angel what ever it reminds me of. See if someone else can see the resemblance. Just watching the clouds move along in the sky is relaxing also.

Stargazing is as old as the stars probably. The Library is a good source to find a book identifying the different constellations. Take a blanket, a pillow and a flashlight into the yard along with a book to identify the stars and use the light to read the book by. A telescope is really nice but that costs money we are talking free stuff here. The stars and moon hold such interesting information. It is truly amazing. Find out for yourselves, its fun.

Go to an old cemetery and see if you can find your last name and other names such as your mother's maiden name. It is nice to take an elderly person along who may be able to give you bits of family history. Take a notepad and write down the information. Compare that information with records you have access to. I know some people do not like to go to cemeteries, others will find it interesting.

Drive along a country road; try to identify the animals seen along the way. The Great Smoky Mountains are homes to many different kinds of animals. Some of those are; the deer, bear, raccoon, opossum, skunk, wild boar, ground hog, turkey, quail, pheasant, ducks, geese, rabbits, squirrels, fox, wildcat or bobcat, cougar. There are many kinds of birds and other fowl. Owls are even seen during the day at times. Keep a record, add to it year after year or trip after trip. Great fun.

Go for a hike, walk only on marked trails if you are not familiar with the area, and never walk alone. The Appalachian Trail goes from Georgia to Maine. I have never walked the whole trail or even plan too, but I have hiked on the trail. It is very easy to get on the trail, hike a few miles, turn and go back the way you came or have someone meet you at a destination point if you are familiar with the area. Get a map and read all information posted along the trail. Take precautions, never assume anything. It's fun and it's free.

Dangle your feet in a cool creek, be careful, and watch out for slippery rocks. A thin film of green on a rock is as slick as ice. Shallow streams are idea for wading and splashing. Take a picnic, have a great time! Go with children and just watch the fun if you do not wish to get in the water, you might just get wet with no effort on your part at all. Children love to splash water on every one and every thing in sight. Watch white water rafters, canoers or kyiakers go down the river be sure to park off the road at designated stops.

Look for a rainbow when the sun comes out after a rain. (Playing in the rain is still fun.) On rare occasions I have seen a double or triple rainbow, of course I didn't have a camera. Sunsets are beautiful; take a late evening drive and your camera. You may end up with a beautiful picture.

Parks and recreational areas are often free for general use. Get permission to use the playground at a church or school for a day, invite others to join in the fun. Wet a large piece of plastic with the water hose, watch the children have a ball slidding on the plastic. If you are real brave wet the grass and done the kids in old clothing turn them loose to slide on the grass, then hose them off.

The possibilities are endless, have fun FREE.

DID YOU KNOW?

****

People used to plant by the signs of the moon. My parents believed in this whole heartedly and Mama still does. The signs change every few days and are named after parts of the body. The moon goes through four phases every month.

Some things done according to the signs; ******

Cut hair on the new moon to promote growth. Men's haircuts last longer if cut on the full moon. Hair grows slower.

Plant vines when signs are in the arms such as cucumbers and runner beans.

Wean a baby when the signs are in the knees, this works for bottle, breast or passie.

Don't plant when the moon is new   ********

Lots of vine but fruit will be few.

Do not plant potatoes or tomatoes when the signs are in the feet. Little toes will grow on them. I wonder if the last part of the name means anything? Toes

The same produce listed above will grow extra parts if planted when the signs are in the privates. Boy? girls?

Do not use salt to pickle when the signs are in the feet or bowels, the pickles will be stinky!!!!!!!!!!!!!

A good time to make pickles is when the signs are in the thighs, knees or legs. I have ruined five gallons of pickles by not going by the signs. I now make sure the signs are "right".

Candy will hold less moisture if made when the moon is full, such as divinity and hard candies. The same works for homemade soaps.

If you want to kill pest weeds or keep shrubs from growing sprouts when cut, cut them down when the dark nights of August appear. They will not come back. You do not have to cut at night. (This advice came from Joe Kinsland, printed in memory of Joe) It is true. Be careful pruning any shrubs during this time.

* For Planting Pumpkins *
Plant in May vines run away
Plant in June fruit comes too soon
Plant in July and you will see why.

Country Firecrackers Place green Mountain Laurel or Ivey on a campfire and listen to the little firecracker presentation.

Popular wood makes a loud pop at times when burning, and will pop out of the fire. I wonder if that is why the name ?

Locust wood makes the best fence posts, the wood lasts longer in the ground, doesn't rote easily. Locost makes good heating wood,it burns slowly.

Sourwood trees make the best sled runners. They grow with a curve. Often times you can find two of the same size growing close by each other.

Hickory is long burning and makes the preferred ashes for making hominy and soap.

Birds that reveal their name by their call are the Whippoorwill and the Bob White.

The Hoot Owl and Bob White calls are mocked by hunters as a signal to each other.

You have heard the saying: "That's what they said but that isn't what they meant."

Here are some examples

He went over yander. (over there)
He brung his gun (brought)

Howje do (how did you do)?

Put the dishes in the zink (sink)

Ranch the dishes (rinse)

I toted a load of wood. (carried)

Fetch me a drank (bring me a drink)

Wash you years (ears)

Don't pint your finger (point)

She packed her child every where. (carried)

He ruk the leaves.(raked)

My lag hurts (leg)

I want ags for breakfast (eggs)

I went to the krek (creek)

I drink through a quill (straw)

The ware got me.(wire)

Build a big far (fire)

He teld a story (told)

Whered he go(where did he go)

Wuz he thar (was he there) ?

Can'tye see (can you not see)?

I storden away (stored them)

Ain't ye going (are you not going)

Ital be ok(it will)

He kilt it (killed it)

Right smart (a good amount)

Some names and how people pronounced them long ago.

Ella was Eller

Stella was Stellar

Emma was Emmer

Lula was Luler

Lela was Lellar

Blanch was Blanj

Ada was Ader

Iris was Arce

Irene was Arene

Other sayings

Did you busser (kiss her)

Sparking meant courting or dating

Spiff up meant to dress up.

Embrace means to hug

Lent money meant to loan money

Trashy people had bad moral habits

No account means no good

Ruint means ruined

Runt was the smallest pig or other baby animal

Grumble and growl means to argue

Bile means boil

Burnt for burned

Spiled for spoiled

Puke for vomit

Stake for fence post

Younder means over there

Bretches were pants

Planks were boards.

Howdy do is How do you do?

Each day of the week was set aside for a particular task.

Washing on Monday

Ironing on Tuesday

Mending on Wednesday

Churning on Thursday

Cleaning on Friday

Baking on Saturday

Rest and Worship on Sunday

WILD PLANTS AND SOME OF THEIR USES

DO NOT EAT ANY WILD BERRIES OR MAKE TEA FROM ANY TREE ROOTS OR LEAVES UNLESS YOU ARE SURE OF THIER IDENITY. Some people may be sensitive to plants that other people are not. Use with caution. Buy a good identifying book of eatable plants and wild flowers, or check out a source from the local Library.

Wild plants that I have personally used:

Blackberries

Raspberries

Strawberries (wood and also common) the wood strawberries are found in these mountains but are not as plentiful or as good tasting as the common strawberries. Tea can be made from either of the leaves. Eat the berries and brew the leaves for tea.

Huckleberries taste different than the wild blueberries.

Gooseberries, these berries are light colored and get ripe in late fall. Great for jam

Dewberries grown closer to the ground than blackberries, sometimes the vine runs on the ground. In Texas these are called blackberries.

Raspberries black & red are delicious. Leaves make a good tea. The purple flowering ones are not as good tasting as the others. The leaves of the purple flowering variety are not recommended for tea.

Buck berries are round smooth black berries that ripen in late fall.

Mountain teaberries are good to eat and the leaves can be chewed.

Mulberries

Fox grapes pick after the frost.

Watercress. Gather young plants, wash in cold water. Use in a garden salad, or with green onions added and pour hot bacon grease with bacon bits over both. You are actually wilting the greens and onions thus the name "kilt". The watercress greens may be boiled and vinegar poured over them. It takes a lot of greens for this method. I prefer them raw.

Branch lettuce, Same as above.

Poke "salat" Boil young shoots and leaves until tender, drain and fry in hot grease with scrambled eggs (my choice) May be eaten with vinegar after boiling (Raymond's choice)

Wild mustard, Gather tender plants wash in cold water. Boil until done, strain off water. Serve hot with vinegar.

Ramps are good fried in potatoes, great deep-fried. Are good raw if you can stand the aftermath (bad breath). Gather in early spring. Wild onions, Use same as onions or ramps. Wild potatoes (boiled). The wild potato tastes like a sweet potato when cooked. The seeds that are formed on the plants above ground tastes like Irish potatoes and looks like miniature potatoes. Wild carrots (Queen Anna's lace) The roots are boiled.

Crab apples make wonderful jelly, no pectin needed........... Persimmons make great jam no pectin needed, (are best if picked after the first frost) use same amount of sugar as prepared fruit or juice after cooking. Boil thirty min. If jams and jellies do not thicken when cooled after thirty minutes of boiling, there probably wasn't enough pectin in the fruit. Reboil with a tablespoon of lemon juice added. If the fruit is really sweet add the lemon juice with the sugar. A tablespoon of butter added with the sugar will prevent the jelly from making a lot of foam.

Dandelion blossom and leaves are good in salad. The root is good for stomach ulcers and mouth sores. I chew the root for a fever blister. A weak tea for the stomach. A strong tea may be toxic. Use with caution.

Wild violets are good in salad and great crystallized for cake decorations. Other etable flowers are Roses, Day Lilies, Margolds, Nasturtiums and Zinnias, these all look pretty in salads and punch.

They are also pretty crystallized for cake, candy or cupcake decorations. When growing up we used raw egg and egg whites in several foods. Today it is not considered safe to use raw egg products. To crystallize flower petals, dip in egg white then dip in sugar. Allow to air dry for twenty four hours. Dip in sugar again. Place a waxed paper under the flowers when placing on cake.

Rose hips are the orange or red fruit that grow after the petals are gone. This fruit is high in vitamin C and can be used to make a tea or jelly. For tea; boil a hand ful of the fruit in a quart of water, strain and sweeten to taste. For jelly, use the same amount of sugar as rose hip tea, boil for thirty minutes. No pectin needed. (Four cups of tea and four cups of sugar.) Wild roses are plentiful here in the mountains. Tame roses have the same value. Do not use petals from commercial grown flowers. Rose water is good to use in soaps and creams.

Passionflower may be eaten raw or made into a tea.

Kudzu blossoms make a beautiful purple jelly, tastes mock grape. Collect the purple cluster blossoms in early fall. Wash in a couple of water changes to be sure to bring out any insects. Use twice the amount of water as blossoms. Four cups of blossoms, eight cups of water. Boil with pot covered for about thirty minutes. Allow to completely cool, overnight is best. Follow grape juice directions to make jelly. Add one tablespoon lemon juice. This printed in memory of Brenda Forbes of Andrews, N. C. She was inventor of Kudzu jelly, or at least the first person I heard of making the jelly. Brenda was a wonderful friend to my sister Dianne.

Pumpkin blossoms are good fried like squash. Rinse blossoms to be sure no insect inside. Use only the male blossoms or you will have no pumpkins at harvest time.

The males are the blossoms without a little pumpkin showing. They just grow on a stem.

OTHER PLANT USES and TIDBITS

Plants are used to make dyes for cloth and basket weaving supplies. My present mother-in –law has educated me on the dyes and such. (Faye Cochran). Thanks Faye! I have actually made these dyes and dyed some material.

Black walnut hulls make a beautiful brown dye.

Yellow root makes a light yellow dye and the root also makes a tea that is good for the tummy. The stuff tastes awful!

Bloodroot makes a bright orange dye.

Pokeberry dyes a pretty purple or magenta depending on the length of time the cloth is soaked in the dye.

Blackberry dyes a darker purple than poke.

Regular tea and coffee dyes to a pretty light beige and browns.

Boil a "good sized amount" of the root or berries in a big pot with water up half way of pot. Add one half to one cup of unidiozed salt to hot dye after the root or berries have been removed. Dip garment or cloth into the dye until desired shade. Rinse in cold water with some white vinegar added. Hang to dry outside. Do not ring out excess water, let drip.

NUTS IN THE WILD FOR FOOD

Black walnut

Hickory nuts

Chinquapin nuts: these are very hard to find now days. But oh, so good!

White oak acorns taste a little bitter and resemble chestnuts in flavor.

Chestnuts are good eaten raw or boiled.

Hazel nuts

Common wood sorrel is good in soaps, hand creams; can also be eaten in salads. Has been held in high regards due to its ability to cure skin cancer. Gather a bunch of the flowering plants. Wash in cool water. Boil for ten or fifteen minutes. Use the liquid for soaking cracked heels. Place the boiled plant in the blender and liquefy. Use a cotton ball to apply to affected skin twice a day. Has relieved itch and rash of poison oak and ivy. It has helped relieve exema and psoriasis. The liquid can be used in place of the water in making soap.

Burdock leaves are good in a salad.

Buttermilk is good to stop yeast infections

Whisky with herbs was used to cure worms, colic, stomach cramping, headaches and induce sleep. Use with caution. Is addictive.

Chickweed is good for cuts and skin disorders per Raymond Cochran and others.

Bull nettle berries help to relieve joint pain, break open the green or yellow berries (in the fall) and rub on skin of painful joint. The root made into a necklace help keep babies from slobbering during teething per Lisa Smith Waldroup (Emma's daughter-in –law).

Elderberry leaves boiled in water is good for skin sores, cuts, scratches and etc.

Poke root boiled has been used for relief of arthritis pain. Both of these remedies came from Kathy Breedlove Cloer. (She is Florence Breedloves daughter).

Lavender oil mixed with water makes a good deodorant, mix three drops per cup of boiled water. Use with a cotton ball. Alcohol on a cotton ball makes a good deodorant too. Lavender blossoms can be soaked in alcohol for a double effect. Lavender flowers can be added to teas lending a beautiful fragrance. The flowers become bitter if steeped too long.

Cucumber juice cools the skin and relieves itching. While in the garden picking corn and other "itchy" produce like okra, pick a cucumber, slice off a section and rub on hands. A cucumber slice is good for the face too. Cucumber soup is good for the tummy on a hot day. Puree a large cucumber in the blended, add one half cup plain yogurt and one half cup of buttermilk. Mix well. Pour into cold cups and top with chopped chives or scallions.

My Uncle Odell Sutton said "Clorox will draw the poising from snakebite sites". He said, "Homemade white liquor would do so too". He had heard his Dad tell about a man who reached into the hiding place to retrieve his jug of whisky and a rattlesnake bit him on the forearm. First the man drank a right smart (quiet a lot) of the whisky and soaked his arm in the rest. The man supposedly did not go to the doctor and lived to tell the story. He took a very long nap too.

A poisonous spider bit my mother and that's what my Grandma had her do. She drank some of the whisky and Grandma soaked a rag with whiskey and. placed it on the site where she was bitten. My Mother was instructed to go to bed for a while. Mama was just fine. She said the site itched for some time but no serious ill effects

My Grandpa Jess Sutton carried a bottle of turpentine with him. He was bitten by a rattlesnake at one time. The story goes like this, "He just turned the turpentine bottle up and placed it over the bite site and you could see the poison going right into the bottle".

My Grandpa didn't go to the doctor.

Lemon juice helps soothe a sore throat. Lemon juice cuts mucous from throat also. Lemon water aids in digestion. Add sugar and you have lemon aide. Lemon, honey and black pepper make a good cough expectant. Equal parts of lemon, honey and whiskey makes a good cough medicine.

Honey is a natural antiseptic first aide remedy for a lot of skin wounds.

Honey is also good on bread with butter, or mixed with peanut butter on bread

Grandma made a salve from balm of Gilead tree buds which she doctored all sorts of skin wounds.

Cornstarch makes a good powder for babies and adults. You can add scents by putting rose petals or lavender blossoms in the cornstarch and leaving it airtight for a couple of days. Sift to remove the flowers.

WHISKEY MAKING INGREDIENTS

Cornmeal cooked in a big pot

With water quiet a lot

Cover and leave to sour

Do not disturb until day four, same hour.

Lots of sugar in a wooden pot.

Add malt corn, not a lot

After five days if no bubbles

Then you have troubles.

Otherwise put all into a very big pot.

Heat to very hot.

Continue to boil

Then run through a coil.

Allow the steam to cool.

Drink sparingly, don't be a fool.

The addiction of white corn liquor

Is very hard to conquer

This poem was derived from whiskey making directions given to me by my Daddy some years ago. I do not promote the drinking of alcohol, however it was a way of life for my ancestors. Making and selling homemade whiskey was illegal then and now, unless you were hired by the Revenuers to provide whisky for legal sale as my Grandpa Charlie Dehart was at one time.

Drinks of old times

Sweet milk…cows milk that wasn't soured. Milk soured quickly without refrigeration

Buttermilk….milk that had soured and had been churned to remove the butter fat.

Milkshake….milk mixed with beaten egg, vanilla and sugar, whip until frothy. Used to increase the appetite and was considered a treat.

Apple juice

Tomato juice

Blackberry juice

Grape juice...Boil the fruit or berries until done, let set several hours and strain through a thin cloth placed over another container to catch the juice. Sweeten as desired for taste.

Home brewed beer

Root beer

Kool aide

Lemon aide

Tea

Coffee

Water (earth juice)

To make fruit leather, puree fruit in a blender. Pour onto a wax paper lined cookie sheet. Allow to dry completely. Roll in wax paper and store in an airtight container. You may speed the process by placing the cookie sheet in a "just barley warm" oven for a couple of hours,

We made Kool-aide ice pops.

Root beer drink was made from a powder sold by a peddler. Sassafras tea could be made by boiling the root adding sugar and leaving to ferment. Tastes sort of like root beer. Sassafras tea is delicious in cold weather as hot tea. In warm weather as a cold tea.

Blackberry juice was used to calm an upset stomach. This juice would stay on the stomach when everything else would "come back up"

Catnip tea was used to stop colic in babies and adults; also promotes sleep. May be habit forming, is reported to be a relative of the marijuana plant. Boil the leaves, strain. Add a little sugar and given to baby by one teaspoon at a time.

Home brewed beer was used to calm nausea and headaches, if used too often and too much it can cause the same. Place one teaspoon sugar in one half cup of home brewed beer, chill or pour over ice. Drink and go to bed. (My Grandma Pearl's remedy).

Yellow root tea is good for stomach pains such as ulcers and pain from taking aspirin. Boil the root in two cups of water. Remove the root. Drink hot or cold. This stuff tastes awful! But it does soothe the stomach. (This is the same yellow root used to make dye for cloth or baskets).

Aloe Vera plant is good to treat burns & sunburns. The juice is taken orally for stomach problems and general healthy well being. I use the aloe juice in making soaps and hand creams.

Rabbit tobacco would make you dizzy when rolled in a paper and smoked. This would also get you in trouble with Mama, but Daddy was the one we heard talking about smoking it. If chewed and swallowed it would make you vomit, so would the juice of snuff or tobacco swallowed. The juice of snuff or chewed tobacco was used to bring relief from stings and insect bites.

Lemon Aide; Boil six cups of sugar in a quart of water until well dissolved. Add one quart of bottled lemon juice. Pour into a two-gallon container and fill with ice water.

Stir well. Float thin lemon slices on top. (To make one gallon use half of this recipe.)

Raspberry Iced Tea; Brew enough tea to make one gallon. Mix two cups of sugar in the hot tea until sugar is well dissolved. Mix in two cups of strained raspberry juice. A pack of Kool-Aide powdered drink mix may be substituted for the juice. A little more sugar may be needed. Crystal Light can also be used for the Kool aide. Add ice water to make one gallon.

Other flavors of tea may be made by adding different flavors of Crystal Light dry mix or Kool aide or juices. Play with mixing until you find what you like.

Spice Wood leaves are good as a tea. Pour boiling water over leaves and allow to steep for ten to fifteen minutes. Sweeten with honey, molasses or corn syrup. Spice Wood leaves make a wonderful aroma in the house. Gather leaves and place in dresser drawers or closets.

Spice wood was used to cook wild meats. Break up pieces of stems and place over the meat. Use leaves too.

SECTION NINE:
RECIPES

RECIPES

Coconut Bon-bons

6 large marshmallows cut into small chunks

One cup of coconut put in the blender and chop fine

One forth cup white corn syrup

One half-teaspoon vanilla or almond flavoring

Melt marshmallows and syrup over medium heat, stirring well. Remove from heat. Add the coconut and flavoring stir well. Allow cooling enough to handle. Shape into ¾ inch balls. Makes 20. Cool for thirty minutes in frig.

Coating

Melt one pound of milk chocolate coating in top of a double boiler. Dip balls in coating with a tooth pick, cool on wax paper.

For molded bon-boons

Use candy mold for choc covered cherries

Drop ½ tsp of chocolate coating into a mold. Use a clean unused artist paintbrush to paint the chocolate into the mold. Continue with all the molds. Place coconut balls into molds and pour chocolate coating over the ball. Allow to cool. Place in refrigerator for a few minutes before removing from mold by turning upside down and tapping on the back of mold.

Use pastel candy coating for a variety of colors. Store candy in an air tight container.

(This was my Daddy's favorite candy; he got to where chocolate bothered him. He liked the colored coating.)

My Mom's black walnut cake

Using a two-layer yellow cake mix, as directed on box. Add one half to three forth cup of chopped fine black walnuts to mix just before putting in the pan. Cook at 300° one hour. Test with a tooth pick. Cook a little longer if not done. My Mama starts this cake in a cold oven. Put the pan in and turn on the heat.

Make icing according to directions on powdered sugar box. Add one half cup crushed black walnuts. Mix well and spread onto cake. One layer at a time. Cover top and sides. Better if made a day ahead.

Black Walnut pound cake by Gladys Payne's recipe (In loving memory of Gladys Payne)

1 cup of butter, ½ cup shortening, 5 eggs, 3 cups plain flour, one cup milk, 1 cup black walnuts, 3 cups sugar, ½ tsp salt 1 tsp baking powder 1 tsp vanilla

Beat butter and shortening together, gradually add sugar; cream mixture until light and fluffy. Beat in eggs one at a time. Sift together the dry ingredients and add alternating with milk and vanilla to creamed mixture. Add nuts. Bake in a floured and greased tube pan for 75 minutes at 325° Test with a toothpick.

Glaze: 1 cup sifted powdered sugar, 2 tbs butter 6 tbs cream, ½ tsp vanilla, and ½ cup chopped fine black walnuts. Cream p. sugar and butter add cream, vanilla and walnuts, mix well. Pour over warm cake after removing cake from tube pan. (Gladys was a first cousin to my Daddy. I never can get my cake to taste like hers did.)

Sunday Morning Chocolate Gravy

In a large fry pan melt one stick of butter, two cups sugar, four or five tablespoons coco powder in one half cup water. Remove pan from the stove. Stir together two cups milk and one half cup flour (if plain flour add a dash of salt). Stir until no lumps left. Pour into the pan with sugar mixture. Bring to a boil. cook two minutes. stir constantly. Serve with hot biscuits and butter.

Fried Yeast Donuts

Dissolve two packages dry yeast in one half cup barely warm water. Scald ½ cup milk. combine milk with 1/3 cup butter, 1/3 cup sugar, one teaspoon salt; cool to barely warm. Add one cup plain flour stir well. Beat in two eggs and yeast mixture. Stir in three more cups of flour. Stir well. Place into a greased warm bowl, turn to coat all of dough. Let stand for one hour. Punch down and turn onto a floured surface. Roll out to one half inch thick, cut with a donut cutter, let rise one half hour. Heat oil to 350º. Drop a few donuts at a time into hot oil. Turn only once. Donuts will sometimes turn on thier own. Cook about two minutes. Drain on paper towel. (We drained on a brown paper bag) Drop warm donuts into a brown bag with powdered sugar, coat evenly. Lift out with a fork. Place on wax paper to cool. Eat warm or cold. These were a lot of fun to make and more fun to eat. They were a real treat!

Old Time Fudge

4 Cups sugar 1 cup powdered cocoa ¼ teaspoon salt
1 3/4 cup half/half* ¼ cup real butter, no subs 1 tsp vanilla ½ cup nuts

Grease an 8x11 in. pan. Mix all ingredients except butter, vanilla and nuts, in a heavy saucepan. Heat to a rolling boil stirring constantly. Stop stirring. Continue to boil until temp on candy thermometer reaches 234º or 235º. Remove from heat, place butter in center of pan. Do not stir. Cool until luke warm. Add vanilla to melted butter (in the center of pan). Beat with a wooden spoon until thick and gloss is gone. Quickly stir in chopped black walnuts and pour into pan. Work very quickly. Cut when completely cooled by dipping a sharp knife in hot water.

My Mama used to make this fudge for us kids. I would help her beat the fudge with a wooden spoon. That was hard work. This was a real treat for us.

Potato Candy

One pound of powdered sugar.........Mix with enough mashed white potatoes (with out butter or pepper) to barely moisten the sugar. Start with a small bit of potatoes. It doesn't take much potatoes. Roll out on a piece of wax paper. Spread top with peanut butter. Roll up, making roll as long as possible. Cut through roll at ¾ inches, making pinwheels. Dust with dry powdered sugar. Allow to air dry for a couple of hours. This is best if done on a dry day. This was the most common homemade candy when I was a child. Even little kids can have fun making this candy.

Divinity

Make when the moon is full and on a dry day.

Mix ½ cup fine chopped black walnuts, or chopped dried hickory nuts. We dried hickory nuts in a saucepan on the top of the stove. Heat and stir until brown. Use dried black walnuts.

It is important to use dried nuts to reduce any additional moisture from candy. Divinity can be tricky. ½ cup white corn syrup, 2 ½ cups white granulated sugar, ½ cup water, ¼ tsp salt, 1-teaspoon vanilla, 2 egg whites beaten stiff.

Cook sugar, syrup, water and salt to 248°, stirring. Cover and boil three minutes on med heat. Pour half the mixture over the egg whites, beating constantly with a mixer. Cook remaining syrup to 272°. Pour over candy beating constantly. Beat until candy is loosing the gloss and soft peaks form. Add vanilla and nuts. Drop by a tablespoon at a time onto wax paper. Allow to cool store in airtight container after completely cool and air-dried.

Molasses Taffy

Two cups molasses, one tablespoon butter, one cup sugar, a pinch of baking soda. Boil together in a cast iron skillet, stir constantly for about twenty minutes. Allow to cool to touch. Wash, dry and grease hands. Dip out about two tablespoons into hands. Stretch away out and fold over, repeat. This is called pulling. Continue pulling for about five minutes. Make a long rope. Cut into bite size pieces. Complete all candy. Wash hands and roll candy in wax paper individually.

Rice Pudding (Made from leftover rice at breakfast)

Four cups of left over rice, two cups milk with cream. (Half and half works well. We had cows milk with cream.) One half cup sugar, three beaten eggs, one teaspoon vanilla, one cup raisins. Mix well and pour into a 9"X11" baking pan, buttered. Sprinkle cinnamon and sugar on top of rice. Bake at 325° for 40-45 minutes. If making rice pudding from scratch, cook rice according to recipe on box and add the other ingredients listed here.

Oak Cakes (Made from left over oatmeal from breakfast)
Four cups left over oatmeal. If not sweetened already, add one half cup sugar or honey. Mix in three forth cup all purpose flour which has one teaspoon salt and 1/4 teaspoon soda added. Stir in two tablespoons bacon grease and two tablespoons melted butter. Stir well if too dry add a little warm milk to make a soft dough. Roll out on a smooth surface with a half cup rolled oats. Cut into biscuits. Bake in 400° degree oven for about 12 to 15 minutes. May take a little longer. Serve warm or cold.

Applesauce Pudding (from left over biscuits)
Sweeten one quart of applesauce to taste. Add one teaspoon vanilla and sprinkle in some cinnamon. Slice through cold biscuits two or three times depending on thickness. In a clear bowl place a layer of biscuits, cover with applesauce. Repeat with layers of biscuit and applesauce. Applesauce last. Sprinkle a little extra sugar and cinnamon on top . Allow to set for a couple of hours before serving.

Cobblers can also be made from left over biscuits. Boil peaches or fruit of choice with sugar, a little water and a little corn starch. Drop chunks of biscuit into boiling fruit. Cover and simmer five minutes.

Crackling Cornbread;

Three cups self-rising cornmeal, one cup buttermilk, one half cup water, one cup crackling chips. (Cracklings saved from rendering hog fat.) Stir all ingredients together. Pour into a greased cast iron skillet. Bake in a hot oven about twenty minutes. Eat while hot.

This was included in with my Christmas card from Birdell Sparks a couple of years ago. Last year I included it in with the few cards I sent. I want to share it with you.

Here is a list of folks I know, all written in a book. And every year at Christmas time I go and take a look. That is when I realize that the names are a part, not of the book they are written in, but of my very heart. For each name stands for someone who has touched my life at sometime. And in the meeting they've become the "Rhythm of the Rhyme". I really feel I am composed of each remembered name. While you may not be aware of feeling quiet the same, My life is much better than it was before you came. For once you have known someone, the years cannot erase the memory of a pleasant word or a friendly face. So never think my Christmas cards are just a mere routine of names upon a list, forgotten in between. For when I send a

Christmas card that is addressed to you, It is because you are on that list of folks I'm indebted to. Whether I have known you for many years or few, in some ways you have had a part in shaping things that I do. So every year when Christmas comes around I just realize a new that the biggest gift God can give (other than giving His son as our Savior) is knowing folks like you.

SECTION TEN:
POEMS

RAYMOND *MY BEST FRIEND*

You are my rainbow
God sent you to me when my life was at a low.
Right from the start
I knew you would hold my heart.
Your wit and charm
Made me feel safe from harm.
Your laughter was contagious
Sometimes down-right outrageous.

When others are down on their luck
You do not hesitate to hand over a buck.
A kinder heart could not be found
Even if you look the whole world round.
Always a kind word to others given
Your reward is waiting in heaven.

When I get in a tizzy
Yelling until I make myself dizzy
You remain calm and undisturbed
I wonder if I have made my voice heard.

You calmly say "it will be alright"
Things will be ok when viewed in a different light
Now and then you instigate a little mischief
Never letting-on that it came from you, yourself.
To others life you add spice.
I am proud to be your wife.

Love Bonnie

TO MY AUNT EDNA

From the time I was born
I was treated as yourn

I was only four
When I started camping at your door.
I liked it so much that I came back for more.

If I was at naught
and really got caught,
I got a spanking without a thought.
Yet only seldom were any tears brought.

The things you made for us to eat,
Nowhere in the world could they be beat.
They were oh so pretty as well as sweet.

The skirts you made for us to wear,
Sears & Roebuck had none to compare.
The pleats were so neat and square.
We held our heads high in the air.

If a child could have more than one mother,
Then no doubt you would be my other.

Back then if she was out of snuff
Life became pretty tuff.

In-between the gum and cheek
You could sometimes peek
One would see the awful stuff.
Only one bee sting was enough
Please give me some of that wonderful snuff

There is one thing of which I need to repent
I locked you in the barn, over an hour you spent.
Your face took on a very reddish tint.
Grandma was worried, yet I gave no hint.
So here today under this tent
Please forgive me, I really do repent.
Happy Birthday Aunt Edna I love you.
This was written for Aunt Edna's eightieth birthday.

DAVID TROY PARTON

On May 25th
God gave us a special gift
It's a boy! It's a BOY!
He has been named David Troy

As blue as the skies are his eyes
In the wee morning hours only Mama hears his cries
Oh watch that child eat
And look what feet!

As he grows he gets round and plump
When he tries to walk he falls on his rump.

A few years gone by, through the house David ran
Hollering "catch me Daddy if you can"
Now you are twelve, Oh my
Tell me where did the time fly?

You stand so slim and tall
Will you grow more by the Fall?
In a short time you will be old enough to drive a car
Don't forget what you have been taught and who you are.

Treat others with respect and care
Always trust in God, He your burden will bear.

I love you. David Troy
You are a mighty fine boy!

Love Grandma Bonnie

MELLANIE

Mellanie oh Mell-anie
Where oh where can she be?
You have the cutest little nose
It looks like the new bud of a rose.

You were born before your due time
At month six instead of the usual nine.
Your little legs are slow to run
But that doesn't keep you from having fun

Your eyes are as shiny as a star.
Your new glasses make you see better near and far.
A sweeter girl is not to be found
Even if you search the whole world round.

You have a mighty fine older brother
Who loves you better than all other
You hold all with your charm
Never meaning to cause anyone harm.

Everywhere you go you spread cheer
You will always be so dear.

Mellanie I love you
Grandma Bonnie Lou

MAYSON

My Granddaughter Mayson
Is always running and chasing
After any creeping thing
Or any fluttering wing.

Lizards that run along a fence
Their swift legs are their only defense
Frogs are her fav-orite
Catching one is a pure delight

Turtles are so much fun
A name is given to every single one.
To see a snake is a big thrill
Unaware of their potential to kill.

To catch a big fish
Is her one and only wish
To watch for a baby rabbit
Is an every day habit.

With out stretched arms she will try
To catch every butterfly that flutters by.
For all animals she has a love
They are a gift to us from God above.

Mayson I love you
Grandma Bonnie Lou

DANIEL

At the summers end
A new life began
A healthy baby boy
He is alive, not a toy
Playing with him could be great fun
He kept his Mom on the run
Bottles to fix
For the formula mix

My goodness watch him grow.
Look how he has changed so.
Long arms and legs
Looks like his body is built on pegs.
A few years later
The change was even greater.
He stands a tall young man
Ride a 4-wheeler, He sure can.

Pretty soon the car keys
Hand them over, Dad please
Don't even look at a girl
Allow a few more years to go by in a whirl.
Always be kind to others
Do not forget to kiss your mother.
Listen close to your dads advice
Ask him to repeat it once or twice.

Always put God first
He will help you through the worst.
Sorry I am not coming your way
Hope you have a very happy birthday!

Love from your Aunt Bonnie

ALYSSA

A sweet little baby girl
Arrived on a snow "flurr"
Dressed all in pink
Cute as a wink.
Dylan is a great older brother
He doesn't want her to go to any other.
Her bottle is a must
Mama is the one to trust
Not old enough to walk
And not big enough to talk.
She is a cuddly little thing
Who coos and tries to sing.
Watch her grow, her clothes are tight.
She changes nearly overnight.
Alyssa is a bundle of joy.
Far more fun than a new toy.

Love Grandma Bonnie

DYLAN

Who is that running and squealing?
Why, that is none other than Dylan.
You are a carbon copy
Of your Dad and Poppy
Look at that pretty smile
We haven't seen you in a while.
Those round plump cheeks
Have gotten cuter in just a couple of weeks.
Quick as the wink of the eye
Dylan can disappear and not even try
He can run on those little legs
And do a magic trick on a plate of eggs.
Water is such a thrill
Even if it does carry a chill.
He likes to splash so very high
That no one can stay dry.
His Papaw adores him
It is visa versa with them.
A bundle of pure joy
A playful boy
Oh Dylan, Dylan

Love Grandma Bonnie

MY GARDEN

As I work in this, my garden, the sod
The very spot many before have trod

This soft dirt under my feet,
Help me Lord to grow something to eat.

The rows are not all straight
The fence doesn't even have a gate.

The wild animals help them self
I hope there will be plenty left

The frisky young deer
Seem to be without fear

The same old Raccoon
He feasts every day before noon.

The spry young Ground Hog
She gets out early even in the fog.

So with all the competition
I hope you see my position

This is my only plea
Please cause the animals to flee

Lead them to the hill
Where they may eat their fill

Before I am overcome with anger
Over my garden that is in danger.

TO SONYA BARKER

For some time we have been together
As prayer Mother and prayer Daughter
A couple of years have gone by.
Oh, my, how the time does fly.
Many changes have come your way.
Time does not stand still even for a day.
You are a true treasure
Being your prayer Mother is my pleasure
For God your talents use
Any other way and you will loose.
Then you were a Senior in High School
Now, in your second year of College, how cool.
Our relationship is nice
To my life you add spice.
Always keep God first in your life
One day you will make some man a wonderful wife.
From no other
But your prayer Mother.

I Love You
Bonnie Cochran

FOLLOW UP

I saw an ad in a magazine asking for a story, telling an event of long ago that left a lasting impression on ones life. I began to think about the events in my life that did just that. There were many. I settled on Making Butter and Buttermilk because I thought that would be an easy story to tell.

I had just recently applied for early retirement after thirty two years in the medical field as an L.P.N. I now have more hearing loss as a result of complications from a sever throat and ear infection. I wear an amplified hearing device that is set at the highest level. I read lips a lot. Functioning in a hospital setting was a constant struggle before the additional loss of hearing. I opted for early retirement.

The last fifteen years were spent working at Harris Regional Hospital in Sylva N, C. in the Birthing Center. I had a great job working with newborn babies and their families. My co-workers were wonderful, they were very supportive in my struggle with hearing loss. I miss the people that I worked with, Hi Girls! Donna, Carol B., Lee B., Cindy, Lori, Haidee, Andrea, Tori, Carol S., Denise, Tammy, Janice, Peggy, Cynthia, Heather, Lytisha, Maggie, Cindy N. And the rest, also all the girls from M/B and Third floor. The Medical Staff was aware of my hearing loss and each made sure to "speak up" so I would understand them. I could just look at some of the girls and they knew I had not heard what was said to me and they would repeat it for me. I appreciate all of the courtesy shown to me at the hospital. Dr. Douglas and Dr, Gehring have truly made a difference in my life. Thank you all.

I wrote the story listed above. The encouragement that I received from my husband Raymond, my two brothers Marvin and Charles Sutton and Charles's wife Jennifer, and my cousin Emma Waldroup, inspired me to write this book. Each one, after reading the story said, "you need to write a book" I had never written a story for publication before.

One of my favorite scriptures is "I am thy God; I will strengthen thee; yea, I will help thee…Isaiah 41-10. This was my prayer, "God please bring to my remembrance stories and events to write about". I have said for a long time, "one day I am going to write a book" that day has finally arrived.

The lingo used in these stories is that of the mountains somewhat with modification acquired with every day communication. I do indeed understand mountain talk, and still use words not acceptable outside of the mountains and frowned up on by the educated. The mountain talk has changed due to public education, dyeing of the older generations, and people from other places coming to the mountains in hopes of living in a quieter less congested atmosphere, or for whatever purpose that drew them into these mountains.

I have chosen to live by the old ways of gardening, canning, pickling, drying and storing foods. I am happy with new methods available such as pressure canners without a gauge to watch, freezers, containers used for storage, zip-lock plastic bags, (I thank God for those.) Electric stoves and air conditioning, and also modern transportation. Hot running water is especially important to me. I had to carry water from the spring while growing up, as you read about in this book.

I enjoy camping in the great outdoors with family and friends. My husband and boys are hunters. I prepare Thanksgiving Dinner (in the woods) for twenty- five to thirty people with the help of my husband Raymond and son Chris. My brother-in-law Melvin helps with the cooking when he is off work that week. Others bring drinks and sometimes a dessert. We usually have venison, bear, wild pork and wild turkey. The hunters provide the meat for the meal. I also prepare a regular turkey for those who do not care for the wild meat. We have been camping in all kinds of weather including twelve to eighteen inches of snow. (The snow is my favorite weather even when camping.)

We share our Thanksgiving Dinner with other hunters and encourage any hikers from the Application Trail to join us; some have been delighted with the offer and blessed us by their presence. Several people make a "reservation" from one year to the next. The only consistent thing about the weather at that time of year is that the weather is never the same. We have had beautiful sunny days to cold rain and snow. The nastier the weather the more people we feed. This dinner has sort of become a ministry reaching out to others in love and food.

This past year we were unable to carry on the tradition due to my father's illness. We did prepare the meal and go on a Thanksgiving Picnic close to the usual place

I want my children and grandchildren, nieces, nephews, cousins, future generations, and any other interested ones to have knowledge of growing foods and "putting up" foods for the winter. I want them to have directions to make things of old. I would like to keep ways of yesteryears alive. I hope this book will help to do that.

I want to share my faith and my love for our Lord and Savior Jesus Christ with others.

May God bless you and yours.

Bonnie Cochran

Printed in the United States
42845LVS00004B/79-510